SELECTED ARTICLES FROM
THE FATHER OF **MODERN
MANAGEMENT THINKING**

the
peter f.
drucker
reader

Harvard Business Review Press

Boston, Massachusetts

The web addresses referenced in this book were live and correct at the time of the book's publication but may be subject to change.

Library of Congress cataloging information forthcoming

ISBN: 978-1-63369-219-0
eISBN: 978-1-63369-220-6

The paper used in this publication meets the requirements of the American National Standard for Permanence of Paper for Publications and Documents in Libraries and Archives Z39.48-1992.

Contents

Introduction

This volume collects the most iconic and influential articles by Peter F. Drucker (1909–2005). To call it a representative sample belies the span and the volume of Drucker's writing—38 articles and 39 books in all. But *The Peter F. Drucker Reader* does provide a useful window onto his thinking and his most enduring lessons about leadership, management, productivity, effectiveness, and, perhaps most important, the relationship of people and societies with their organizations.

Drucker's ideas remain startlingly relevant. He was seemingly prescient. In writing so cogently about the burgeoning phenomenon of the "knowledge worker," he was able to imagine with great accuracy how the balance of power would shift in organizations in the late 20th and early 21st centuries, and how their structure, focus, and purpose would change.

Drucker's writing also shows remarkable range. As a matter of course, Drucker places specific management trends in their historical context, connecting, for example, the motivations of service and knowledge workers with the ideas of Frederick Taylor and Karl Marx. He is equally at home discussing organizational strategy, Japanese road systems, planned product obsolescence, activity-based costing, IT evolutions, the development of the Linotype machine, and the habits of individual World War II commanders.

To understand what Drucker is asking managers and executives to do, however, note his depth as well as his breadth—his remarkable ability to zoom in and out on a subject, his proclivity for connecting synthetic, big-picture thinking with detail-oriented, practical requirements. In his arguments he takes into consideration the whole of society, the organizations within it, the leaders of those organizations, and the individuals who make up the workforce. The "effective" executive Drucker describes as an ideal has this same capacity for zooming in and out, focused as much on the changing world economy as on an upcoming meeting; as concerned for the organization's next big strategic move as for the motivation and productivity of individual employees. It's not that executives need to focus on *everything*—that would hardly be efficient. But to be effective, they must be disciplined about their management of important things both large and seemingly small.

Drucker could state a complex idea simply, clearly, and often briefly. He is recognized as a master of aphorism. Many an executive's PowerPoint has been decorated with pithy quotes from him that ring as true now as they did 40 years ago: "There is nothing so useless as doing efficiently what should not be done at all." "The productivity of work is not the responsibility of the worker but of the manager." "You cannot build performance on weakness. You can build only on strengths."

But to read only his aphorisms is to miss much of his most useful advice. Thus HBR has gathered the Drucker essays that will help you be a truly "effective" executive.

In **"What Makes an Effective Executive,"** Drucker argues that charisma is not, in fact, a necessary factor of leadership. He identifies eight practices that effective leaders follow, ranging from big-picture tasks such as asking themselves, "What is right for the enterprise?" to fundamental managerial skills such as running productive meetings. Taken together, these practices yield the knowledge the executive needs, help translate it into action, and ensure that the whole organization feels responsible and accountable for success.

In **"The Theory of the Business,"** Drucker addresses "what to do"—what some might call business strategy. Beginning with the question of why successful companies stagnate, he homes in on the challenge of matching an organization's priorities and goals with the changing realities of a changing world and then making sure that competencies are in place to achieve them.

The primary responsibility of a manager is to strive for the best possible economic results from the resources currently available, Drucker states in **"Managing for Business Effectiveness."** This requires making a distinction between efficiency and effectiveness: *Efficiency* is about getting the maximum amount done—but *effectiveness* is about getting the best results. Hence Drucker advocates focusing on just those product lines that produce the most revenue (in contrast to the product proliferation we see today). He proposes three steps for managers to determine which they are and act to decrease this clutter.[1]

In **"The Effective Decision,"** Drucker describes an approach for executives facing choices that will impact their entire organizations. He argues that such decisions must not be made quickly, because the best measure of their quality lies not in speed but in whether they are put into action and have a positive effect. His process grapples with the inherent compromise between what is ideal and what is possible—between the big picture of organizational objectives and threats and the quotidian realities of execution.

"Executives spend more time on managing people and making people decisions than on anything else—and they should," Drucker writes in **"How to Make People Decisions."** By looking closely at the practices of George C. Marshall (U.S. Army chief of staff during World War II) and Alfred P. Sloan (who led General Motors for four decades), he draws general principles and outlines steps for making sound people decisions. Here we see precursors of ideas he developed elsewhere—the emphasis on developing the strengths (rather than attending to the weaknesses) of the employee that he brings to the fore in the later "Managing Oneself"; the careful consideration of implementation in the earlier "The Effective Decision." Throughout, Drucker highlights situations in which an employee's failure is the fault of management, of the way the job is built, or of how the person was chosen for it.

"They're Not Employees, They're People" examines the shift to more temporary, impersonal arrangements between people and the organizations they work for, which is ongoing. If "developing talent is business's most important task," as Drucker argues, this shift presents some real dangers. In his exploration of its cultural context, Drucker examines such factors as employment regulations and their impact on small businesses especially, and the rise of knowledge

---

1. This article includes one of the surprisingly few instances in which Drucker exhibits the myopia of his time, citing "older, unmarried women" and "clean-up men on the night shift" as primary sources of employee complaint.

work. He warns corporate leaders that however it evolves, "in a knowledge workforce, the system must serve the worker."

Echoes of this idea can be seen throughout Drucker's writings, in which he pragmatically considers that workers' needs are just as integral to the overall corporate system as executives'. For about a century after industrialization, for example, increased economic productivity necessarily came from increased manufacturing and logistics outputs. By the late 20th century, however, many more people were employed in knowledge and service work than in industry, and Drucker recognized that it was in those sectors that any meaningful new productivity gains would need to be made. He discusses this in **"The New Productivity Challenge"** in the context of class warfare and its 19th-century Industrial Revolution origins and concludes that a partnership between employee and manager is a requirement for raising productivity.

Nonprofit management is not often held up as an exemplar for corporate leaders. Yet in **"What Business Can Learn from Nonprofits,"** Drucker argues that nonprofits are leading the way in the motivation and productivity of knowledge workers and are stronger than most for-profit organizations in their strategy and board effectiveness.

In **"The New Society of Organizations,"** Drucker defines the relationship of the organization to society at large. Disagreeing with Milton Friedman that the only responsibility of business is its own economic performance, he foresees a world that looks to both corporations and nonprofits for cures for its biggest social ills.

"Managing Oneself" has the greatest reach beyond the management literature of all Drucker's work. Applicable and accessible to any professionals—not just executives and managers—it has become so influential perhaps because of the simplicity of the self-reflection it encourages; perhaps because we find a surprising amount to identify with in Drucker's exploration of our strengths and weaknesses; or perhaps because permission to have strengths and weaknesses empowers us in a new way. Indeed, empowerment is the outcome of the piece: It is in our hands to shape our careers and our success.

To Drucker, effectiveness comes from asking "What needs to be done?" rather than just making current operations more efficient.

This kind of work continues to be critical even as entire segments of our economy are automated. As early as 1963, Drucker wrote that "while there is plenty of labor-saving machinery around, no one has yet invented a 'work-saving' machine, let alone a 'think-saving' one." Although big data and analytics are beginning to help us with the question of what needs to be done, his exhortation to make those decisions thoughtfully remains as relevant as ever—to our careers, to our organizations, and to our society.

—The Editors

the
peter f.
drucker
reader

What Makes an Effective Executive

AN EFFECTIVE EXECUTIVE DOES not need to be a leader in the sense that the term is now most commonly used. Harry Truman did not have one ounce of charisma, for example, yet he was among the most effective chief executives in U.S. history. Similarly, some of the best business and nonprofit CEOs I've worked with over a 65-year consulting career were not stereotypical leaders. They were all over the map in terms of their personalities, attitudes, values, strengths, and weaknesses. They ranged from extroverted to nearly reclusive, from easygoing to controlling, from generous to parsimonious.

What made them all effective is that they followed the same eight practices:

- They asked, "What needs to be done?"

- They asked, "What is right for the enterprise?"

- They developed action plans.

- They took responsibility for decisions.

- They took responsibility for communicating.

- They were focused on opportunities rather than problems.

- They ran productive meetings.

- They thought and said "we" rather than "I."

The first two practices gave them the knowledge they needed. The next four helped them convert this knowledge into effective action. The last two ensured that the whole organization felt responsible and accountable.

Get the Knowledge You Need

The first practice is to ask what needs to be done. Note that the question is not "What do I want to do?" Asking what has to be done, and taking the question seriously, is crucial for managerial success. Failure to ask this question will render even the ablest executive ineffectual.

When Truman became president in 1945, he knew exactly what he wanted to do: complete the economic and social reforms of Roosevelt's New Deal, which had been deferred by World War II. As soon as he asked what needed to be done, though, Truman realized that foreign affairs had absolute priority. He organized his working day so that it began with tutorials on foreign policy by the secretaries of state and defense. As a result, he became the most effective president in foreign affairs the United States has ever known. He contained Communism in both Europe and Asia and, with the Marshall Plan, triggered 50 years of worldwide economic growth.

Similarly, Jack Welch realized that what needed to be done at General Electric when he took over as chief executive was not the overseas expansion he wanted to launch. It was getting rid of GE businesses that, no matter how profitable, could not be number one or number two in their industries.

The answer to the question "What needs to be done?" almost always contains more than one urgent task. But effective executives do not splinter themselves. They concentrate on one task if at all possible. If they are among those people—a sizable minority—who work best with a change of pace in their working day, they pick two tasks. I have never encountered an executive who remains effective while tackling more than two tasks at a time. Hence, after asking what needs to be done, the effective executive sets priorities and sticks to them. For a CEO, the priority task might be redefin-

Idea in Brief

Worried that you're not a born leader? That you lack charisma, the right talents, or some other secret ingredient? No need: leadership isn't about personality or talent. In fact, the best leaders exhibit wildly different personalities, attitudes, values, and strengths—they're extroverted or reclusive, easygoing or controlling, generous or parsimonious, numbers or vision oriented.

So what do effective leaders have in common? They get the right things done, in the right ways—by following eight simple rules:

- Ask what needs to be done.
- Ask what's right for the enterprise.
- Develop action plans.
- Take responsibility for decisions.
- Take responsibility for communicating.
- Focus on opportunities, not problems.
- Run productive meetings.
- Think and say "We," not "I."

Using discipline to apply these rules, you gain the knowledge you need to make smart decisions, convert that knowledge into effective action, and ensure accountability throughout your organization.

ing the company's mission. For a unit head, it might be redefining the unit's relationship with headquarters. Other tasks, no matter how important or appealing, are postponed. However, after completing the original top-priority task, the executive resets priorities rather than moving on to number two from the original list. He asks, "What must be done now?" This generally results in new and different priorities.

To refer again to America's best-known CEO: Every five years, according to his autobiography, Jack Welch asked himself, "What needs to be done *now*?" And every time, he came up with a new and different priority.

But Welch also thought through another issue before deciding where to concentrate his efforts for the next five years. He asked himself which of the two or three tasks at the top of the list he himself was best suited to undertake. Then he concentrated on that task; the others he delegated. Effective executives try to focus on

Idea in Practice

Get the Knowledge You Need

Ask what needs to be done. When Jack Welch asked this question while taking over as CEO at General Electric, he realized that dropping GE businesses that couldn't be first or second in their industries was essential—not the overseas expansion he had wanted to launch. Once you know what must be done, identify tasks you're best at, concentrating on one at a time. After completing a task, reset priorities based on new realities.

Ask what's right for the enterprise. Don't agonize over what's best for owners, investors, employees, or customers. Decisions that are right for your *enterprise* are ultimately right for all stakeholders.

Convert Your Knowledge into Action

Develop action plans. Devise plans that specify *desired results* and *constraints* (is the course of action legal and compatible with the company's mission, values, and policies?). Include *check-in points* and *implications for how you'll spend your time*. And *revise* plans to reflect new opportunities.

Take responsibility for decisions. Ensure that each decision specifies who's accountable for carrying it out, when it must be implemented, who'll be affected by it, and who must be informed. Regularly review decisions, especially hires and promotions. This enables you to correct

jobs they'll do especially well. They know that enterprises perform if top management performs—and don't if it doesn't.

Effective executives' second practice—fully as important as the first—is to ask, "Is this the right thing for the enterprise?" They do not ask if it's right for the owners, the stock price, the employees, or the executives. Of course they know that shareholders, employees, and executives are important constituencies who have to support a decision, or at least acquiesce in it, if the choice is to be effective. They know that the share price is important not only for the shareholders but also for the enterprise, since the price/earnings ratio sets the cost of capital. But they also know that a decision that isn't right for the enterprise will ultimately not be right for any of the stakeholders.

poor decisions before doing real damage.

Take responsibility for communicating. Get input from superiors, subordinates, and peers on your action plans. Let each know what information you need to get the job done. Pay equal attention to peers' and superiors' information needs.

Focus on opportunities, not problems. You get results by exploiting opportunities, not solving problems. Identify changes inside and outside your organization (new technologies, product innovations, new market structures), asking "How can we exploit this change to benefit our enterprise?" Then match your best people with the best opportunities.

Ensure Companywide Accountability

Run productive meetings. Articulate each meeting's purpose (Making an announcement? Delivering a report?). Terminate the meeting once the purpose is accomplished. Follow up with short communications summarizing the discussion, spelling out new work assignments and deadlines for completing them. General Motors CEO Alfred Sloan's legendary mastery of meeting follow-up helped secure GM's industry dominance in the mid-twentieth century.

Think and say "We," not "I." Your authority comes from your organization's trust in you. To get the best results, always consider your organization's needs and opportunities before your own.

This second practice is especially important for executives at family owned or family run businesses—the majority of businesses in every country—particularly when they're making decisions about people. In the successful family company, a relative is promoted only if he or she is measurably superior to all nonrelatives on the same level. At DuPont, for instance, all top managers (except the controller and lawyer) were family members in the early years when the firm was run as a family business. All male descendants of the founders were entitled to entry-level jobs at the company. Beyond the entrance level, a family member got a promotion only if a panel composed primarily of nonfamily managers judged the person to be superior in ability and performance to all other employees at the same level. The same rule was observed for a century in the highly successful British family business J. Lyons & Company (now part of a major conglomerate) when it dominated the British food-service and hotel industries.

Asking "What is right for the enterprise?" does not guarantee that the right decision will be made. Even the most brilliant executive is human and thus prone to mistakes and prejudices. But failure to ask the question virtually guarantees the *wrong* decision.

Write an Action Plan

Executives are doers; they execute. Knowledge is useless to executives until it has been translated into deeds. But before springing into action, the executive needs to plan his course. He needs to think about desired results, probable restraints, future revisions, check-in points, and implications for how he'll spend his time.

First, the executive defines desired results by asking: "What contributions should the enterprise expect from me over the next 18 months to two years? What results will I commit to? With what deadlines?" Then he considers the restraints on action: "Is this course of action ethical? Is it acceptable within the organization? Is it legal? Is it compatible with the mission, values, and policies of the organization?" Affirmative answers don't guarantee that the action will be effective. But violating these restraints is certain to make it both wrong and ineffectual.

The action plan is a statement of intentions rather than a commitment. It must not become a straitjacket. It should be revised often, because every success creates new opportunities. So does every failure. The same is true for changes in the business environment, in the market, and especially in people within the enterprise—all these changes demand that the plan be revised. A written plan should anticipate the need for flexibility.

In addition, the action plan needs to create a system for checking the results against the expectations. Effective executives usually build two such checks into their action plans. The first check comes halfway through the plan's time period; for example, at nine months. The second occurs at the end, before the next action plan is drawn up.

Finally, the action plan has to become the basis for the executive's time management. Time is an executive's scarcest and most precious resource. And organizations—whether government agencies, businesses, or nonprofits— are inherently time wasters. The action plan will prove useless unless it's allowed to determine how the executive spends his or her time.

Napoleon allegedly said that no successful battle ever followed its plan. Yet Napoleon also planned every one of his battles, far more meticulously than any earlier general had done. Without an action plan, the executive becomes a prisoner of events. And without check-ins to reexamine the plan as events unfold, the executive has no way of knowing which events really matter and which are only noise.

Act

When they translate plans into action, executives need to pay particular attention to decision making, communication, opportunities (as opposed to problems), and meetings. I'll consider these one at a time.

Take responsibility for decisions

A decision has not been made until people know:

- the name of the person accountable for carrying it out;

- the deadline;

- the names of the people who will be affected by the decision and therefore have to know about, understand, and approve it—or at least not be strongly opposed to it—and

- the names of the people who have to be informed of the decision, even if they are not directly affected by it.

An extraordinary number of organizational decisions run into trouble because these bases aren't covered. One of my clients, 30 years ago, lost its leadership position in the fast-growing Japanese market because the company, after deciding to enter into a joint venture with a new Japanese partner, never made clear who was to inform the purchasing agents that the partner defined its specifications in meters and kilograms rather than feet and pounds—and nobody ever did relay that information.

It's just as important to review decisions periodically—at a time that's been agreed on in advance—as it is to make them carefully in the first place. That way, a poor decision can be corrected before it does real damage. These reviews can cover anything from the results to the assumptions underlying the decision.

Such a review is especially important for the most crucial and most difficult of all decisions, the ones about hiring or promoting people. Studies of decisions about people show that only one-third of such choices turn out to be truly successful. One-third are likely to be draws—neither successes nor outright failures. And one-third are failures, pure and simple. Effective executives know this and check up (six to nine months later) on the results of their people decisions. If they find that a decision has not had the desired results, they don't conclude that the person has not performed. They conclude, instead, that they themselves made a mistake. In a well-managed enterprise, it is understood that people who fail in a new job, especially after a promotion, may not be the ones to blame.

Executives also owe it to the organization and to their fellow workers not to tolerate nonperforming individuals in important jobs. It may not be the employees' fault that they are underperforming, but even so, they have to be removed. People who have failed in a new job should be given the choice to go back to a job at their former level and salary. This option is rarely exercised; such people, as a rule, leave voluntarily, at least when their employers are U.S. firms. But the very existence of the option can have a powerful effect, encouraging people to leave safe, comfortable jobs and take risky new assignments. The organization's performance depends on employees' willingness to take such chances.

A systematic decision review can be a powerful tool for self-development, too. Checking the results of a decision against its expectations shows executives what their strengths are, where they need to improve, and where they lack knowledge or information. It shows them their biases. Very often it shows them that their decisions didn't produce results because they didn't put the right people on the job. Allocating the best people to the right positions is a crucial, tough job that many executives slight, in part because the best people are already too busy. Systematic decision review also shows executives their own weaknesses, particularly the areas in which they are simply incompetent. In these areas, smart executives don't make decisions or take actions. They delegate. Everyone has such areas; there's no such thing as a universal executive genius.

Most discussions of decision making assume that only senior executives make decisions or that only senior executives' decisions matter. This is a dangerous mistake. Decisions are made at every level of the organization, beginning with individual professional contributors and frontline supervisors. These apparently low-level decisions are extremely important in a knowledge-based organization. Knowledge workers are supposed to know more about their areas of specialization—for example, tax accounting—than anybody else, so their decisions are likely to have an impact throughout the company. Making good decisions is a crucial skill at every level. It needs to be taught explicitly to everyone in organizations that are based on knowledge.

Take responsibility for communicating

Effective executives make sure that both their action plans and their information needs are understood. Specifically, this means that they share their plans with and ask for comments from all their colleagues—superiors, subordinates, and peers. At the same time, they let each person know what information they'll need to get the job done. The information flow from subordinate to boss is usually what gets the most attention. But executives need to pay equal attention to peers' and superiors' information needs.

We all know, thanks to Chester Barnard's 1938 classic *The Functions of the Executive*, that organizations are held together by information rather than by ownership or command. Still, far too many executives behave as if information and its flow were the job of the information specialist—for example, the accountant. As a result, they get an enormous amount of data they do not need and cannot use, but little of the information they do need. The best way around this problem is for each executive to identify the information he needs, ask for it, and keep pushing until he gets it.

Focus on opportunities

Good executives focus on opportunities rather than problems. Problems have to be taken care of, of course; they must not be swept under the rug. But problem solving, however necessary, does not produce results. It prevents damage. Exploiting opportunities produces results.

Above all, effective executives treat change as an opportunity rather than a threat. They systematically look at changes, inside and outside the corporation, and ask, "How can we exploit this change as an opportunity for our enterprise?" Specifically, executives scan these seven situations for opportunities:

- an unexpected success or failure in their own enterprise, in a competing enterprise, or in the industry;

- a gap between what is and what could be in a market, process, product, or service (for example, in the nineteenth century, the paper industry concentrated on the 10% of each tree that became wood pulp and totally neglected the possibilities in the remaining 90%, which became waste);

- innovation in a process, product, or service, whether inside or outside the enterprise or its industry;

- changes in industry structure and market structure;

- demographics;

- changes in mind-set, values, perception, mood, or meaning; and

- new knowledge or a new technology.

Effective executives also make sure that problems do not overwhelm opportunities. In most companies, the first page of the monthly management report lists key problems. It's far wiser to list opportunities on the first page and leave problems for the second page. Unless there is a true catastrophe, problems are not discussed in management meetings until opportunities have been analyzed and properly dealt with.

Staffing is another important aspect of being opportunity focused. Effective executives put their best people on opportunities rather than on problems. One way to staff for opportunities is to ask each member of the management group to prepare two lists every six months—a list of opportunities for the entire enterprise and a list of the best-performing people throughout the enterprise. These are discussed, then melded into two master lists, and the best people are matched with the best opportunities. In Japan, by the way, this matchup is considered a major HR task in a big corporation or government department; that practice is one of the key strengths of Japanese business.

Make meetings productive

The most visible, powerful, and, arguably, effective nongovernmental executive in the America of World War II and the years thereafter was not a businessman. It was Francis Cardinal Spellman, the head of the Roman Catholic Archdiocese of New York and adviser to several U.S. presidents. When Spellman took over, the diocese was bankrupt and totally demoralized. His successor inherited the leadership position in the American Catholic church. Spellman often said that during his waking hours he was alone only twice each day, for 25 minutes each time: when he said Mass in his private chapel after getting up in the morning and when he said his evening prayers before going to bed. Otherwise he was always with people in a meeting, starting at breakfast with one Catholic organization and ending at dinner with another.

Top executives aren't quite as imprisoned as the archbishop of a major Catholic diocese. But every study of the executive workday has found that even junior executives and professionals are with other people—that is, in a meeting of some sort—more than half of every business day. The only exceptions are a few senior researchers. Even a conversation with only one other person is a meeting. Hence, if they are to be effective, executives must make meetings productive. They must make sure that meetings are work sessions rather than bull sessions.

The key to running an effective meeting is to decide in advance what kind of meeting it will be. Different kinds of meetings require different forms of preparation and different results:

- *A meeting to prepare a statement, an announcement, or a press release.* For this to be productive, one member has to prepare a draft beforehand. At the meeting's end, a preappointed member has to take responsibility for disseminating the final text.

- *A meeting to make an announcement—for example, an organizational change.* This meeting should be confined to the announcement and a discussion about it.

- *A meeting in which one member reports.* Nothing but the report should be discussed.

- *A meeting in which several or all members report.* Either there should be no discussion at all or the discussion should be limited to questions for clarification. Alternatively, for each report there could be a short discussion in which all participants may ask questions. If this is the format, the reports should be distributed to all participants well before the meeting. At this kind of meeting, each report should be limited to a preset time—for example, 15 minutes.

- *A meeting to inform the convening executive.* The executive should listen and ask questions. He or she should sum up but not make a presentation.

- *A meeting whose only function is to allow the participants to be in the executive's presence.* Cardinal Spellman's breakfast and dinner meetings were of that kind. There is no way to make these meetings productive. They are the penalties of rank. Senior executives are effective to the extent to which they can prevent such meetings from encroaching on their workdays. Spellman, for instance, was effective in large part because he confined such meetings to breakfast and dinner and kept the rest of his working day free of them.

Making a meeting productive takes a good deal of self-discipline. It requires that executives determine what kind of meeting is appropriate and then stick to that format. It's also necessary to terminate the meeting as soon as its specific purpose has been accomplished. Good executives don't raise another matter for discussion. They sum up and adjourn.

Good follow-up is just as important as the meeting itself. The great master of follow-up was Alfred Sloan, the most effective business executive I have ever known. Sloan, who headed General Motors from the 1920s until the 1950s, spent most of his six working days a week in meetings—three days a week in formal committee meetings with a set membership, the other three days in ad hoc meetings with individual GM executives or with a small group of executives. At the beginning of a formal meeting, Sloan announced the meeting's purpose. He then listened. He never took notes and he rarely spoke except to clarify a confusing point. At the end he summed up, thanked the participants, and left. Then he immediately wrote a short memo addressed to one attendee of the meeting. In that note, he summarized the discussion and its conclusions and spelled out any work assignment decided upon in the meeting (including a decision to hold another meeting on the subject or to study an issue). He specified the deadline and the executive who was to be accountable for the assignment. He sent a copy of the memo to everyone who'd been present at the meeting. It was through these memos—each a small masterpiece—that Sloan made himself into an outstandingly effective executive.

Effective executives know that any given meeting is either productive or a total waste of time.

Think and Say "We"

The final practice is this: Don't think or say "I." Think and say "we." Effective executives know that they have ultimate responsibility, which can be neither shared nor delegated. But they have authority only because they have the trust of the organization. This means that they think of the needs and the opportunities of the organization before they think of their own needs and opportunities. This one may sound simple; it isn't, but it needs to be strictly observed.

We've just reviewed eight practices of effective executives. I'm going to throw in one final, bonus practice. This one's so important that I'll elevate it to the level of a rule: *Listen first, speak last.*

Effective executives differ widely in their personalities, strengths, weaknesses, values, and beliefs. All they have in common is that they get the right things done. Some are born effective. But the demand is much too great to be satisfied by extraordinary talent. Effectiveness is a discipline. And, like every discipline, effectiveness *can* be learned and *must* be earned.

Originally published in June 2004. Reprint R0406C

The Theory of the Business

NOT IN A VERY LONG TIME—not, perhaps, since the late 1940s or early 1950s—have there been as many new major management techniques as there are today: downsizing, outsourcing, total quality management, economic value analysis, benchmarking, reengineering. Each is a powerful tool. But, with the exceptions of outsourcing and reengineering, these tools are designed primarily to do differently what is already being done. They are "how to do" tools.

Yet "what to do" is increasingly becoming the central challenge facing managements, especially those of big companies that have enjoyed long-term success. The story is a familiar one: a company that was a superstar only yesterday finds itself stagnating and frustrated, in trouble and, often, in a seemingly unmanageable crisis. This phenomenon is by no means confined to the United States. It has become common in Japan and Germany, the Netherlands and France, Italy and Sweden. And it occurs just as often outside business—in labor unions, government agencies, hospitals, museums, and churches. In fact, it seems even less tractable in those areas.

The root cause of nearly every one of these crises is not that things are being done poorly. It is not even that the wrong things are being done. Indeed, in most cases, the *right* things are being done—but fruitlessly. What accounts for this apparent paradox? The assumptions on which the organization has been built and is being run no longer fit reality. These are the assumptions that shape any organization's behavior, dictate its decisions about what to do and what not to do, and define what the organization considers meaningful results. These assumptions are about markets. They are about identifying customers and competitors, their values and behavior. They are about technology and its dynamics, about a company's strengths and weaknesses. These assumptions are about what a company gets paid for. They are what I call a company's *theory of the business.*

Every organization, whether a business or not, has a theory of the business. Indeed, a valid theory that is clear, consistent, and focused is extraordinarily powerful. In 1809, for instance, German statesman and scholar Wilhelm von Humboldt founded the University of Berlin on a radically new theory of the university. And for more than 100 years, until the rise of Hitler, his theory defined the German university, especially in scholarship and scientific research. In 1870, Georg Siemens, the architect and first CEO of Deutsche Bank, the first universal bank, had an equally clear theory of the business: to use entrepreneurial finance to unify a still rural and splintered Germany through industrial development. Within 20 years of its founding, Deutsche Bank had become Europe's premier financial institution, which it has remained to this day in spite of two world wars, inflation, and Hitler. And, in the 1870s, Mitsubishi was founded on a clear and completely new theory of the business, which within 10 years made it the leader in an emerging Japan and within another 20 years made it one of the first truly multinational businesses.

Similarly, the theory of the business explains both the success of companies like General Motors and IBM, which have dominated the U.S. economy for the latter half of the twentieth century, and the challenges they have faced. In fact, what underlies the current malaise of so many large and successful organizations worldwide is that their theory of the business no longer works.

———

Whenever a big organization gets into trouble—and especially if it has been successful for many years—people blame sluggishness, complacency, arrogance, mammoth bureaucracies. A plausible

Idea in Brief

In his thirty-first article for HBR, Peter F. Drucker argues that what underlies the current malaise of so many large and successful organizations worldwide is that their theory of the business no longer works. The story is a familiar one: a company that was a superstar only yesterday finds itself stagnating and frustrated, in trouble and, often, in a seemingly unmanageable crisis. The root cause of nearly every one of these crises is not that things are being done poorly. It is not even that the wrong things are being done. Indeed, in most cases, the right things are being done—but fruitlessly.

What accounts for this apparent paradox? The assumptions on which the organization has been built and is being run no longer fit reality. These are the assumptions that shape any organization's behavior, dictate its decisions about what to do and what not to do, and define what an organization considers meaningful results. These assumptions are what Drucker calls a company's theory of the business.

Every organization, whether a business or not, has a theory of the business. The theory of the business explains both the successes of companies like General Motors and IBM, which have dominated the U.S. economy for the latter half of the twentieth century, and the challenges they have faced.

Some theories of the business are so powerful that they last for a long time. But being human artifacts, they don't last forever, and today they rarely last for very long at all. Eventually, every theory of the business becomes obsolete and then invalid. When a theory shows the first signs of becoming obsolete, it is time to start rethinking the theory, with the clear premise that our historically transmitted assumptions no longer suffice.

explanation? Yes. But rarely the relevant or correct one. Consider the two most visible and widely reviled "arrogant bureaucracies" among large U.S. companies that have recently been in trouble.

Since the earliest days of the computer, it had been an article of faith at IBM that the computer would go the way of electricity. The future, IBM knew, and could prove with scientific rigor, lay with the central station, the ever-more-powerful mainframe into which a huge number of users could plug. Everything—economics, the logic of information, technology—led to that conclusion. But then, suddenly, when it seemed as if such a central-station, mainframe-based information system was actually coming into existence, two young men came up with the first personal computer. Every computer maker knew that the PC was absurd. It did not have the memory, the database, the speed, or the computing ability necessary to succeed. Indeed, every computer maker knew that the PC had to fail—the conclusion reached by Xerox only a few years earlier, when its research team had actually built the first PC. But when that misbegotten monstrosity—first the Apple, then the Macintosh—came on the market, people not only loved it, they bought it.

Every big, successful company throughout history, when confronted with such a surprise, has refused to accept it. "It's a stupid fad and will be gone in three years," said the CEO of Zeiss upon seeing the new Kodak Brownie in 1888, when the German company was as dominant in the world photographic market as IBM would be in the computer market a century later. Most mainframe makers responded in the same way. The list was long: Control Data, Univac, Burroughs, and NCR in the United States; Siemens, Nixdorf, Machines Bull, and ICL in Europe; Hitachi and Fujitsu in Japan. IBM, the overlord of mainframes with as much in sales as all the other computer makers put together and with record profits, could have reacted in the same way. In fact, it *should* have. Instead, IBM immediately accepted the PC as the new reality. Almost overnight, it brushed aside all its proven and time-tested policies, rules, and regulations and set up not one but two competing teams to design an even simpler PC. A couple of years later, IBM had become the world's largest PC manufacturer and the industry standard setter.

There is absolutely no precedent for this achievement in all of business history; it hardly argues bureaucracy, sluggishness, or arrogance. Yet despite unprecedented flexibility, agility, and humility, IBM was floundering a few years later in both the mainframe and the PC business. It was suddenly unable to move, to take decisive action, to change.

The case of GM is equally perplexing. In the early 1980s—the very years in which GM's main business, passenger automobiles, seemed almost paralyzed—the company acquired two large businesses:

Hughes Electronics and Ross Perot's Electronic Data Systems. Analysts generally considered both companies to be mature and chided GM for grossly overpaying for them. Yet, within a few short years, GM had more than tripled the revenues and profits of the allegedly mature EDS. And ten years later, in 1994, EDS had a market value six times the amount that GM had paid for it and ten times its original revenues and profits.

Similarly, GM bought Hughes Electronics—a huge but profitless company involved exclusively in defense—just before the defense industry collapsed. Under GM management, Hughes has actually increased its defense profits and has become the only big defense contractor to move successfully into large-scale nondefense work. Remarkably, the same bean counters who had been so ineffectual in the automobile business—30-year GM veterans who had never worked for any other company or, for that matter, outside of finance and accounting departments—were the ones who achieved those startling results. And in the two acquisitions, they simply applied policies, practices, and procedures that had already been used by GM.

This story is a familiar one at GM. Since the company's founding in a flurry of acquisitions 80 years ago, one of its core competencies has been to "overpay" for well-performing but mature businesses—as it did for Buick, AC Spark Plug, and Fisher Body in those early years—and then turn them into world-class champions. Very few companies have been able to match GM's performance in making successful acquisitions, and GM surely did not accomplish those feats by being bureaucratic, sluggish, or arrogant. Yet what worked so beautifully in those businesses that GM knew nothing about failed miserably in GM itself.

———————

What can explain the fact that at both IBM and GM the policies, practices, and behaviors that worked for decades—and in the case of GM are still working well when applied to something new and different—no longer work for the organization in which and for which they were developed? The realities that each organization actually faces have changed quite dramatically from those that each still assumes it lives with. Put another way, reality has changed, but the theory of the business has not changed with it.

Before its agile response to the new reality of the PC, IBM had once before turned its basic strategy around overnight. In 1950, Univac, then the world's leading computer company, showed the prototype of the first machine designed to be a multipurpose computer. All earlier designs had been for single-purpose machines. IBM's own two earlier computers, built in the late 1930s and 1946, respectively, performed astronomical calculations only. And the machine that IBM had on the drawing board in 1950, intended for the SAGE air defense system in the Canadian Arctic, had only one purpose: early identification of enemy aircraft. IBM immediately scrapped its strategy of developing advanced single-purpose machines; it put its best engineers to work on perfecting the Univac architecture and, from it, designing the first multipurpose computer able to be manufactured (rather than handcrafted) and serviced. Three years later, IBM had become the world's dominant computer maker and standardbearer. IBM did not create the computer. But in 1950, its flexibility, speed, and humility created the computer *industry*.

However, the same assumptions that had helped IBM prevail in 1950 proved to be its undoing 30 years later. In the 1970s, IBM assumed that there was such a thing as a "computer," just as it had in the 1950s. But the emergence of the PC invalidated that assumption. Mainframe computers and PCs are, in fact, no more one entity than are generating stations and electric toasters. The latter, while different, are interdependent and complementary. In contrast, mainframe computers and PCs are primarily competitors. And, in their basic definition of *information*, they actually contradict each other: for the mainframe, information means memory; for the brainless PC, it means software. Building generating stations and making toasters must be run as separate businesses, but they can be owned by the same corporate entity, as General Electric did for decades. In contrast, mainframe computers and PCs probably cannot coexist in the same corporate entity.

IBM tried to combine the two. But because the PC was the fastest growing part of the business, IBM could not subordinate it to the mainframe business. As a result, the company could not optimize the mainframe business. And because the mainframe was still the cash cow, IBM could not optimize the PC business. In the end, the assumption that a computer is a computer—or, more prosaically, that the industry is hardware driven—paralyzed IBM.

GM had an even more powerful, and successful, theory of the business than IBM had, one that made GM the world's largest and most profitable manufacturing organization. The company did not have one setback in 70 years—a record unmatched in business history. GM's theory combined in one seamless web assumptions about markets and customers with assumptions about core competencies and organizational structure.

Since the early 1920s, GM assumed that the U.S. automobile market was homogeneous in its values and segmented by extremely stable income groups. The resale value of the "good" used car was the only independent variable under management's control. High trade-in values enabled customers to upgrade their new-car purchases to the next category—in other words, to cars with higher profit margins. According to this theory, frequent or radical changes in models could only depress trade-in values.

Internally, these market assumptions went hand in hand with assumptions about how production should be organized to yield the biggest market share and the highest profit. In GM's case, the answer was long runs of mass-produced cars with a minimum of changes each model year, resulting in the largest number of uniform yearly models on the market at the lowest fixed cost per car.

GM's management then translated these assumptions about market and production into a structure of semiautonomous divisions, each focusing on one income segment and each arranged so that its highest priced model overlapped with the next division's lowest priced model, thus almost forcing people to trade up, provided that used-car prices were high.

For 70 years, this theory worked like a charm. Even in the depths of the Depression, GM never suffered a loss while steadily gaining market share. But in the late 1970s, its assumptions about the market and about production became invalid. The market was fragmenting into highly volatile "lifestyle" segments. Income became one factor among many in the buying decision, not the only one. At the same time, lean manufacturing created an economics of small scale. It made short runs and variations in models less costly and more profitable than long runs of uniform products.

GM knew all this but simply could not believe it. (GM's union still doesn't.) Instead, the company tried to patch things over. It maintained the existing divisions based on income segmentation, but each division now offered a "car for every purse." It tried to compete with lean manufacturing's economics of small scale by automating the large-scale, long-run mass production (losing some $30 billion in the process). Contrary to popular belief, GM patched things over with prodigious energy, hard work, and lavish investments of time and money. But patching only confused the customer, the dealer, and the employees and management of GM itself. In the meantime, GM neglected its *real* growth market, where it had leadership and would have been almost unbeatable: light trucks and minivans.

A theory of the business has three parts. First, there are assumptions about the environment of the organization: society and its structure, the market, the customer, and technology.

Second, there are assumptions about the specific mission of the organization. Sears, Roebuck and Company, in the years during and following World War I, defined its mission as being the informed buyer for the American family. A decade later, Marks and Spencer in Great Britain defined its mission as being the change agent in British society by becoming the first classless retailer. AT&T, again in the years during and immediately after World War I, defined its role as ensuring that every U.S. family and business have access to a telephone. An organization's mission need not be so ambitious. GM envisioned a far more modest role—as the leader in "terrestrial motorized transportation equipment," in the words of Alfred P. Sloan, Jr.

Third, there are assumptions about the core competencies needed to accomplish the organization's mission. For example, West Point, founded in 1802, defined its core competence as the ability to turn out leaders who deserve trust. Marks and Spencer, around 1930, defined its core competence as the ability to identify, design, and develop the merchandise it sold, instead of as the ability to buy. AT&T, around 1920, defined its core competence as technical leadership that would enable the company to improve service continuously while steadily lowering rates.

The assumptions about environment define what an organization is paid for. The assumptions about mission define what an organization considers to be meaningful results; in other words, they point to how it envisions itself making a difference in the economy and in the society at large. Finally, the assumptions about core competencies define where an organization must excel in order to maintain leadership.

Of course, all this sounds deceptively simple. It usually takes years of hard work, thinking, and experimenting to reach a clear, consistent, and valid theory of the business. Yet to be successful, every organization must work one out.

What are the specifications of a valid theory of the business? There are four.

1. The assumptions about environment, mission, and core competencies must fit reality. When four penniless young men from Manchester, England, Simon Marks and his three brothers-in-law, decided in the early 1920s that a humdrum penny bazaar should become an agent of social change, World War I had profoundly shaken their country's class structure. It had also created masses of new buyers for good-quality, stylish, but cheap merchandise like lingerie, blouses, and stockings—Marks and Spencer's first successful product categories. Marks and Spencer then systematically set to work developing brand-new and unheard-of core competencies. Until then, the core competence of a merchant was the ability to buy well. Marks and Spencer decided that it was the merchant, rather than the manufacturer, who knew the customer. Therefore, the merchant, not the manufacturer, should design the products, develop them, and find producers to make the goods to his design, specifications, and costs. This new definition of the merchant took five to eight years to develop and make acceptable to traditional suppliers, who had always seen themselves as "manufacturers," not "subcontractors."

2. The assumptions in all three areas have to fit one another. This was perhaps GM's greatest strength in the long decades of its ascendancy. Its assumptions about the market and about the optimum manufacturing process were a perfect fit. GM decided in the mid-1920s that it also required new and as-yet-unheard-of core competencies: financial control of the manufacturing process and a theory of capital allocations. As a result, GM invented modern cost accounting and the first rational capital-allocation process.

3. The theory of the business must be known and understood throughout the organization. That is easy in an organization's early days. But as it becomes successful, an organization tends increasingly to take its theory for granted, becoming less and less conscious of it. Then the organization becomes sloppy. It begins to cut corners. It begins to pursue what is expedient rather than what is right. It stops thinking. It stops questioning. It remembers the answers but has forgotten the questions. The theory of the business becomes "culture." But culture is no substitute for discipline, and the theory of the business is a discipline.

4. The theory of the business has to be tested constantly. It is not graven on tablets of stone. It is a hypothesis. And it is a hypothesis about things that are in constant flux—society, markets, customers, technology. And so, built into the theory of the business must be the ability to change itself.

———————

Some theories of the business are so powerful that they last for a long time. But being human artifacts, they don't last forever, and, indeed, today they rarely last for very long at all. Eventually every theory of the business becomes obsolete and then invalid. That is precisely what happened to those on which the great U.S.

businesses of the 1920s were built. It happened to the GMs and the AT&Ts. It has happened to IBM. It is clearly happening today to Deutsche Bank and its theory of the universal bank. It is also clearly happening to the rapidly unraveling Japanese *keiretsu*.

The first reaction of an organization whose theory is becoming obsolete is almost always a defensive one. The tendency is to put one's head in the sand and pretend that nothing is happening. The next reaction is an attempt to patch, as GM did in the early 1980s or as Deutsche Bank is doing today. Indeed, the sudden and completely unexpected crisis of one big German company after another for which Deutsche Bank is the "house bank" indicates that its theory no longer works. That is, Deutsche Bank no longer does what it was designed to do: provide effective governance of the modern corporation.

But patching never works. Instead, when a theory shows the first signs of becoming obsolete, it is time to start thinking again, to ask again which assumptions about the environment, mission, and core competencies reflect reality most accurately—with the clear premise that our historically transmitted assumptions, those with which all of us grew up, no longer suffice.

What, then, needs to be done? There is a need for preventive care—that is, for building into the organization systematic monitoring and testing of its theory of the business. There is a need for early diagnosis. Finally, there is a need to rethink a theory that is stagnating and to take effective action in order to change policies and practices, bringing the organization's behavior in line with the new realities of its environment, with a new definition of its mission, and with new core competencies to be developed and acquired.

Preventive Care. There are only two preventive measures. But, if used consistently, they should keep an organization alert and capable of rapidly changing itself and its theory. The first measure is what I call *abandonment*. Every three years, an organization should challenge every product, every service, every policy, every distribution channel with the question, If we were not in it already, would we be going into it now? By questioning accepted policies and routines, the organization forces itself to think about its theory. It forces itself to test assumptions. It forces itself to ask: Why didn't this work, even though it looked so promising when we went into it five years ago? Is it because we made a mistake? Is it because we did the wrong things? Or is it because the right things didn't work?

Without systematic and purposeful abandonment, an organization will be overtaken by events. It will squander its best resources on things it should never have been doing or should no longer do. As a result, it will lack the resources, especially capable people, needed to exploit the opportunities that arise when markets, technologies, and core competencies change. In other words, it will be unable to respond constructively to the opportunities that are created when its theory of the business becomes obsolete.

The second preventive measure is to study what goes on outside the business, and especially to study *noncustomers*. Walk-around management became fashionable a few years back. It *is* important. And so is knowing as much as possible about one's customers—the area, perhaps, where information technology is making the most rapid advances. But the first signs of fundamental change rarely appear within one's own organization or among one's own customers. Almost always they show up first among one's noncustomers. Noncustomers always outnumber customers. Wal-Mart, today's retail giant, has 14% of the U.S. consumer-goods market. That means 86% of the market is noncustomers.

In fact, the best recent example of the importance of the noncustomer is U.S. department stores. At their peak some 20 years ago, department stores served 30% of the U.S. nonfood retail market. They questioned their customers constantly, studied them, surveyed them. But they paid no attention to the 70% of the market who were not their customers. They saw no reason why they should. Their theory of the business assumed that most people who could afford to shop in department stores did. Fifty years ago, that assumption fit reality. But when the baby boomers came of age, it ceased to be valid. For the dominant group among baby boomers—women in educated two-income families—it was not money that determined where to shop. Time was the primary factor, and this generation's women could not afford to spend their time shopping in department stores. Because department stores looked only at their own customers, they did not recognize this change until a few years ago. By then, business was already drying up. And it was too late to get the baby boomers back. The department stores learned the hard way that although being customer driven is vital, it is not enough. An organization must be market driven too.

Early Diagnosis. To diagnose problems early, managers must pay attention to the warning signs. A theory of the business always becomes obsolete when an organization attains its original objectives. Attaining one's objectives, then, is not cause for celebration; it is cause for new thinking. AT&T accomplished its mission to give every U.S. family and business access to the telephone by the mid-1950s. Some executives then said it was time to reassess the theory of the business and, for instance, separate local service—where the objectives had been reached—from growing and future businesses, beginning with long-distance service and extending into global telecommunications. Their arguments went unheeded, and a few years later AT&T began to flounder, only to be rescued by antitrust, which did by fiat what the company's management had refused to do voluntarily.

Rapid growth is another sure sign of crisis in an organization's theory. Any organization that doubles or triples in size within a fairly short period of time has necessarily outgrown its theory. Even Silicon Valley has learned that beer bashes are no longer adequate for communication once a company has grown so big that people have to wear name tags. But such growth challenges much deeper assumptions, policies, and habits. To continue in health, let alone grow, the organization has to ask itself again the questions about its environment, mission, and core competencies.

There are two more clear signals that an organization's theory of the business is no longer valid. One is unexpected success—whether one's own or a competitor's. The other is unexpected failure—again, whether one's own or a competitor's.

At the same time that Japanese automobile imports had Detroit's Big Three on the ropes, Chrysler registered a totally unexpected success. Its traditional passenger cars were losing market share even faster than GM's and Ford's were. But sales of its Jeep and its new minivans—an almost accidental development—skyrocketed. At the time, GM was the leader of the U.S. light-truck market and unchallenged in the design and quality of its products, but it wasn't paying any attention to its light-truck capacity. After all, minivans and light trucks had always been classified as commercial rather than passenger vehicles in traditional statistics, even though most of them are now being bought as passenger vehicles. However, had it paid attention to the success of its weaker competitor, Chrysler, GM might have realized much earlier that its assumptions about both its market and its core competencies were no longer valid. From the beginning, the minivan and light-truck market was not an income-class market and was little influenced by trade-in prices. And, paradoxically, light trucks were the one area in which GM, 15 years ago, had already moved quite far toward what we now call lean manufacturing.

Unexpected failure is as much a warning as unexpected success and should be taken as seriously as a 60-year-old man's first "minor" heart attack. Sixty years ago, in the midst of the Depression, Sears decided that automobile insurance had become an "accessory" rather than a financial product and that selling it would therefore fit its mission as being the informed buyer for the American family. Everyone thought Sears was crazy. But automobile insurance became Sears's most profitable business almost instantly. Twenty years later, in the 1950s, Sears decided that diamond rings had become a necessity rather than a luxury, and the company became the world's largest— and probably most profitable—diamond retailer. It was only logical for Sears to decide in 1981 that investment products had become consumer goods for the American family. It bought Dean Witter and moved its offices into Sears stores. The move was a total disaster. The U.S. public clearly did not consider its financial needs to be "consumer products." When Sears finally gave up and decided to run

Dean Witter as a separate business outside Sears stores, Dean Witter at once began to blossom. In 1992, Sears sold it at a tidy profit.

Had Sears seen its failure to become the American family's supplier of investments as a failure of its theory and not as an isolated incident, it might have begun to restructure and reposition itself ten years earlier than it actually did, when it still had substantial market leadership. For Sears might then have seen, as several of its competitors like J.C. Penney immediately did, that the Dean Witter failure threw into doubt the entire concept of market homogeneity—the very concept on which Sears and other mass retailers had based their strategy for years.

Cure. Traditionally, we have searched for the miracle worker with a magic wand to turn an ailing organization around. To establish, maintain, and restore a theory, however, does not require a Genghis Khan or a Leonardo da Vinci in the executive suite. It is not genius; it is hard work. It is not being clever; it is being conscientious. It is what CEOs are paid for.

There are indeed quite a few CEOs who have successfully changed their theory of the business. The CEO who built Merck into the world's most successful pharmaceutical business by focusing solely on the research and development of patented, high-margin breakthrough drugs radically changed the company's theory by acquiring a large distributor of generic and nonprescription drugs. He did so without a "crisis," while Merck was ostensibly doing very well. Similarly, a few years ago, the new CEO of Sony, the world's best-known manufacturer of consumer electronic hardware, changed the company's theory of the business. He acquired a Hollywood movie production company and, with that acquisition, shifted the organization's center of gravity from being a hardware manufacturer in search of software to being a software producer that creates a market demand for hardware.

But for every one of these apparent miracle workers, there are scores of equally capable CEOs whose organizations stumble. We can't rely on miracle workers to rejuvenate an obsolete theory of the business any more than we can rely on them to cure other types of serious illness. And when one talks to these supposed miracle workers, they deny vehemently that they act by charisma, vision, or, for that matter, the laying on of hands. They start out with diagnosis and analysis. They accept that attaining objectives and rapid growth demand a serious rethinking of the theory of the business. They do not dismiss unexpected failure as the result of a subordinate's incompetence or as an accident but treat it as a symptom of "systems failure." They do not take credit for unexpected success but treat it as a challenge to their assumptions.

They accept that a theory's obsolescence is a degenerative and, indeed, life-threatening disease. And they know and accept the surgeon's time-tested principle, the oldest principle of effective decision making: A degenerative disease will not be cured by procrastination. It requires decisive action.

Originally published in September–October 1994. Reprint 94506

Managing
for Business
Effectiveness

WHAT IS THE FIRST DUTY—and the continuing responsibility—of the business manager? *To strive for the best possible economic results from the resources currently employed or available.* Everything else managers may be expected to do, or may want to do, rests on sound economic performance and profitable results over the next few years. Even such lofty management tasks as assessing corporate social responsibilities and cultural opportunities are not exempt from this presupposition. And certainly not exempt, by and large, are the individual manager's *own rewards*—money and position.

Accordingly, all business executives spend much, if not all, of their time on the problems of short-run economic performance. They concern themselves with costs and pricing, with scheduling and selling, with quality control and customer service, with purchasing and training. Furthermore, the vast array of tools and techniques available to the modern manager deal to a great extent with managing *today's* business for today's and tomorrow's economic performance. This is the subject matter of 90 out of any 100 books in the business library, and (conservatively) of 90 out of any 100 reports and studies produced within businesses.

No Time for Clichés

Despite all this attention, few managers I know are greatly impressed with their own performance in this work. They want to know how to organize for the task; how to tell the important from the time-wasting, the potentially effective from the merely frustrating. Despite the flood of data and reports threatening to inundate the manager today, he gets only the vaguest generalities. Such banalities as "low costs" or "high profit margins" are bandied about as answers to the question: What *really* determines economic performance and results in this particular business that I work for?

Even in the boom times of a "seller's market," managing for economic performance tends to be a source of constant frustration. And as soon as times return to normal and markets become competitive again, managing for economic performance tends to generate such confusion, pressure, and anxiety that the decisions made are most unlikely to be the right ones, even for short-run results, let alone for the company's future.[1]

What we need are not more or better tools—we have already many more than any single business (let alone any single manager) can use. What we need are simple concepts—some crude rules of thumb—that will help organize the job by answering:

- Just what is the manager's job?

- What is the major problem in it?

- What is the principle for defining this problem and for analyzing it?

Misplaced emphasis

I do not propose to give here a full-blown "science of management economics," if only because I have none to give. Even less do I intend to present a magic formula, a "checklist" or "procedure" which will do the job for the manager. For his job is *work*—very hard, demanding, risk-taking work. And while there is plenty of laborsaving machinery around, no one has yet invented a "work-saving" machine, let alone a "think-saving" one.

Idea in Brief

Productive business managers are those who obtain optimum economic results from the available resources. A series of primary steps, which have proven to be highly effective for managers in actual business situations, include: (1) analyzing the facts in terms of opportunities and costs of products, as well as the contributions of staff, and the "cost streams"; (2) allocating resources, according to projected results, by analyzing present and future resource allocations; and (3) prioritizing decisions with respect to area of greatest potential for opportunity and results.

But I do claim that we know how to organize the job of managing for economic effectiveness and how to do it with both direction and results. The answers to the three key questions above are known, and have been known for such a long time that they should not surprise anyone.

1. *What is the manager's job?* It is to direct the resources and the efforts of the business toward opportunities for economically significant results. This sounds trite—and it is. But every analysis of actual allocation of resources and efforts in business that I have ever seen or made showed clearly that *the bulk of time, work, attention, and money first goes to "problems" rather than to opportunities, and, secondly, to areas where even extraordinarily successful performance will have minimal impact on results.*

2. *What is the major problem?* It is fundamentally the confusion between effectiveness and efficiency that stands between doing the right things and doing things right. *There is surely nothing quite so useless as doing with great efficiency what should not be done at all.* Yet our tools—especially our accounting concepts and data—all focus on efficiency. What we need is (1) a way to identify the areas of effectiveness (of possible significant results), and (2) a method for concentrating on them.

3. *What is the principle?* That, too, is well-known—at least as a general proposition. Business enterprise is not a phenomenon of nature but one of society. In a social situation, however,

33

events are not distributed according to the "normal distribution" of a natural universe (that is, they are not distributed according to the U-shaped Gaussian curve). *In a social situation a very small number of events—10% to 20% at most—account for 90% of all results, whereas the great majority of events account for 10% or less of the results.*

This is true in the marketplace. A handful of customers out of many thousands produce the bulk of the orders; a handful of products out of hundreds of items in the line produce the bulk of the volume; and so on. This is true of markets, end uses, and distributive channels. It is equally true of sales efforts: a few salesmen, out of several hundred, always produce two-thirds or more of all new business. It is true in the plant: a handful of production runs account for most of the tonnage. It is true of research: a few men in the laboratory produce all the important innovations, as a rule.

It also holds true for practically all personnel "problems": the great bulk of the grievances always come from a few places or from one group of employees (for example, from the older, unmarried women or from the clean-up men on the night shift), as does the great bulk of absenteeism, of turnover, of suggestions under a suggestion system, and of accidents. As studies at the New York Telephone Company have shown, this is true even in respect to employee sickness.

Revenue $ versus Cost $

The importance that this simple statement about "normal distribution" has for managing a business has been grasped by all too few businessmen. It means, first: *while 90% of the results are being produced by the first 10% of events, 90% of the costs are being increased by the remaining and result-less 90% of events.*

In other words, costs, too, are a "social phenomenon." If we put it into mathematical language, we see that the "normal distribution curve" of business events is a hyperbola with the results plotted along the plus half, and the costs along the minus half of the curve. Thus, results and costs stand in inverse relationship to each other.

And now, translated back into common language, *economic results are, by and large, directly proportionate to revenue, while costs are directly proportionate to number of transactions.* The only exceptions to this are the purchased materials and parts that go directly into the final product. For example:

- To get a $50,000 order costs no more, as a rule, than to get a $500 order; certainly it does not cost 100 times as much.

- To design a new product that does not sell is as expensive as to design a "winner."

- It costs just as much to do the paper work for a small order as for a large one—the same order entry, production order, scheduling, billing, collecting, and so on.

- It even costs just as much, as a rule, to actually make the product, to package it, and to transport it for a small order as for a large one. Even labor is a "fixed" cost today over any period of time in most manufacturing industries (and in all services) rather than a cost fluctuating with volume. Only purchased materials and parts are truly "variable" costs.

Furthermore, there is the implication that, *"normally," revenues and efforts will allocate themselves to the 90% of events that produce practically no results.* They will allocate themselves according to the *number of events* rather than according to results. In fact, the most expensive and potentially most productive resources (i.e., highly trained people) will misallocate themselves the worst. For the pressure exerted by the bulk of transactions is fortified by the person's pride in doing the difficult—whether productive or not.

This has been proved by every single study made; it is, in other words, supported both by principle and by concrete experience. Let me give some examples:

- A large engineering company prided itself on the high quality and reputation of its technical service group, which contained several hundred expensive men. The men were indeed first-rate. But analysis of their allocation showed clearly that they, while working hard, contributed little. Most of them worked on the "interesting" problems—especially those of the very small customers—problems which, even if solved, produced little, if any, business. The automobile industry is the company's major customer and accounts for almost one-third of all purchases. But few technical service people within anyone's memory had even set foot in the engineering department or the plant of an automobile company. "General Motors and Ford don't need us; they have their own people," was their reaction.

- Similarly, in many companies salesmen are misallocated. The largest group of salesmen (and especially the most effective ones) are usually put on the products that are "hard to sell," either because they are "yesterday's products" or because they are "also rans" which managerial vanity desperately is trying to make into "winners." Tomorrow's important products very rarely get the sales effort required. And the product that has sensational success in the market—and which, therefore, ought to be pushed all-out—tends to be slighted. "It is doing all right without extra effort, after all," is the common conclusion.

- Research departments, design staffs, market development efforts, even advertising efforts have been shown to be allocated the same way in lots of companies—by transaction rather than by results, by what is difficult rather than by what is productive, by yesterday's problems rather than by today's and tomorrow's opportunities!

Unaccountable accounting

"Revenue money" and "cost money," to put it dramatically, are not automatically the same "money stream." Revenue produces the wherewithal for the costs, of course. But unless management constantly seeks to direct these costs into revenue-producing activities, they will tend to allocate themselves *by drift* into "nothing-producing" activities.

One major reason why managers do not, as a rule, understand this fact is their mistaken identification of *accounting* data and analysis with *economic* data and business analysis.[2] The accountant has to allocate to all products those costs that are not actually and physically tied to a particular unit of production. Today, one way or another, the great bulk of the costs—the 60% to 70% that are not purchased materials and parts—are, consequently, allocated, rather than truly "direct," costs.

Now the only way the accountant can allocate costs is in a way that is proportionate to volume rather than proportionate to the number of transactions. Thus, $1 million in volume produced in one order—or in one product—carries the same cost as $1 million in volume produced by 1 million individual orders or by 50 different production runs.

Similarly the accountant is concerned with the cost per unit of output rather than with the costs of a product. His focus is on profit margin rather than on profit stream—which is, of course, profit margin multiplied by turnover. Finally, the accountant does not classify costs by the economic activity to which they pertain. Instead, he classifies by organizational or geographic locus (e.g., "manufacturing" or "plant"), or by legal—or legalistic—categories (e.g., "payroll").

I am well aware of the work done on these and related problems of accounting theory and practice—indeed I owe whatever understanding of accounting I have to this work and to the accountants engaged in it. But it will be years before the results of this work will penetrate accounting practice, let alone change the way businessmen use or misuse accounting data.

Rifle Approach

More important than the reasons *why* we have not drawn the right conclusions is: What *are* the right conclusions? What line of action will produce the best possible economic results and performance from the resources available to a business? Let us begin by setting some guidelines:

1. Economic results require that managers concentrate their efforts on the smallest number of products, product lines,

services, customers, markets, distribution channels, end uses, and so on which will produce the largest amount of revenue. Managers must minimize the attention devoted to products which produce primarily costs, because their volume is too small or too splintered.

2. Economic results require also that staff efforts be concentrated on the very few activities that are capable of producing truly significant business results—with as little staff work and staff effort as possible spent on the others.

3. Effective cost control requires a similar concentration of work and efforts on those very few areas where improvement in cost performance will have significant impact on business performance and results—that is, on those areas where a relatively *minor* increase in efficiency will produce a *major* increase in economic effectiveness.

4. Managers must allocate resources, especially *high-grade human resources*, to activities which provide opportunities for high economic results.

Unpardonable profligacy

No wonder so many businesses did poorly the moment the "seller's market" was over. The wonder, rather, is that they did not do worse. For most businesses—those abroad as well as those in this country—operate in direct opposition to every one of the four well-known rules I have just spelled out.

Instead of product concentration we have product clutter. Remember how it used to be fashionable to attack industry, especially U.S. industry, for its "deadening standardization"? Then, a few years ago, it became fashionable to attack industry for its "planned obsolescence." If only there *were* any validity to either of these charges!

Most businesses—today's large U.S. corporations are perhaps the worst offenders—pride themselves on being willing and able to supply *any* "specialty," to satisfy *any* demand for variety, even to stimulate such demands in the first place. And any number of businesses boast that they never, of their own free will, abandon a product. As a result, most large companies typically end up with thousands of items in their product line—and all too frequently fewer than 20 really "sell." However, these 20 items or less have to contribute revenues to carry the costs of the 9,999 nonsellers.

Indeed, the basic problem of U.S. competitive strength in the world economy today may well be product clutter. If properly costed, the main lines in most of our industries will prove to be fully competitive, despite our high wage rates and our high tax burden. But we fritter away our competitive advantage in the volume products by subsidizing an enormous array of "specialties," of which only a few recover their true cost. This, at least, is what I have found in such industries as steel and aluminum. And in electronics the competitive advantage of the Japanese portable transistor radio rests on little more than the Japanese concentration on a few models in this one line—as against the uncontrolled plethora of barely differentiated models in the U.S. manufacturers' lines.

We are similarly profligate in this country with respect to staff activities. Our motto seems to be, "Let's do a little bit of everything"—personnel research, advanced engineering, customer analysis, international economics, operations research, public relations, and so on. As a result, we build enormous staffs, and yet do not concentrate enough effort in any one area to get very far. Nor do we know what to do to remedy the situation. The common way to control costs is still the one everybody knows to be ineffectual if not destructive: the "across-the-board-cut" by 15%. We have not really made a serious attempt to manage resources and pinpoint our efforts. Things are left to drift along.

Three Giant Steps

Criticizing is easy; anyone can find fault. Readers have every right to say, at this point, "Just how can we go about doing a better job of managing?" Even if I had all the answers—and I do not—an article would not be long enough for me to offer a satisfactory reply. This would require a book; and even then every company would *still* have to work out the methods best suited to its own affairs.

So, if readers will bear with me, I will present a series of steps—sketched out only in the lightest of strokes—that I have found to be highly effective in actual business situations, at least as first approaches. Specifically:

Step 1. Analysis—Here the manager has to know the facts. He needs to identify:

- The opportunities and true costs of products.

- The potential contributions of different staff activities.

- The economically significant cost centers.

Step 2. Allocation—Here the manager has to allocate resources according to results anticipated. For this, he needs to know:

- How resources are allocated now.

- How resources should be allocated in the future to support activities of greatest opportunity.

- What steps are necessary to get from what *is* to what *ought to be.*

Step 3. Decision—The manager must be prepared to take the most painful step of all—that of deciding on those products, staff activities, or cost areas that breed clutter rather than bring opportunity and results. Naturally, productive resources of any magnitude or potential should never be allocated to these. But which should be abandoned altogether? Which should be maintained at a minimum effort? Which could be changed into major opportunities, and what would it cost to make such a change?

Analyzing the Facts

In the analysis stage, the first job is to take an unsentimental look at the product line. All the standard questions should be asked about each product: its volume, market standing, market outlook, and so on. There is, however, one new key question: What does the product contribute? What does a comparison of its revenue with its true costs show?

In this analysis, revenue should be defined as total sales dollars less costs of purchased materials and supplies. And true costs should be estimated on the basis of this (most probable) assumption—that the real cost of a product is the proportion of the total cost of the business that corresponds to the ratio between the number of transactions (orders, production runs, service calls, and the like) needed to obtain the product's revenue and total number of similar transactions in the business—less, again, materials and parts costs. Since this is cumbersome, let me give a concrete example:

A company had annual revenues of $68 million, after taking out costs of materials and parts purchased. Total costs of the business— materials and parts excepted—were $56 million.

Product A showed revenues of $12 million a year. It required, however, 24% of the total number of transactions—measured in this case by invoices. Its true costs were, therefore, calculated to be $13.5 million a year, which meant a negative contribution, in sharp contrast to the "official" profit margin of almost 12% that the accounting figures showed. (This, by the way, is typical for "yesterday's product," which has either lost the main customers or can be held in the market only by uneconomic efforts.)

Product B, by contrast, despite an "unsatisfactory" profit margin of only 3%, showed a net revenue contribution of almost $4 million— the largest single contribution to profit. It went in sizable orders to a small number—about 50—of substantial customers.

As the examples show, this analysis looks at *all the products* of a business rather than at one at a time. This by itself is unusual and rarely done.

While the product breakdown is normally the most important and most revealing analysis, customers, markets, distribution channels, and end uses all need to be analyzed similarly in respect to their present and their anticipated contributions.

Staff contribution

The questions to be asked in this analysis call for managerial judgment rather than for economic data. Here is a list of queries I have found useful:

- In what areas would excellence really have an extraordinary impact on the economic results of our business, to the point where it might transform the economic performance of the entire business?

- In what areas would poor performance threaten to damage economic performance, greatly or at least significantly?

- In what areas would it make little difference whether we perform excellently or poorly?

- What results have been attained by the work done in the area? How do these compare with the results promised or expected?

- What results can realistically be expected for the future—and how far ahead is the future?

Cost centers

The object here is to isolate those areas of the business where a concentration of cost control efforts will pay off. Rather than describe methods by which this analysis can be carried out, I would like to show the results of an actual study made by a substantial manufacturer of nationally distributed consumer goods (see the exhibit, "The consumer's dollar—where it goes"). For convenience, the figures for the various cost centers are given in absolute terms, but each is an approximation. In the actual study, the summary of "total costs," for example, ranged from 90% to 94%, while other figures had ranges somewhat less extreme.

The only innovation as to methods used by the manufacturer is that "cost" is defined (as it must be when one talks about economics) as what the customer spends on the product. In other words, this analysis looks at the entire economic process as one cost

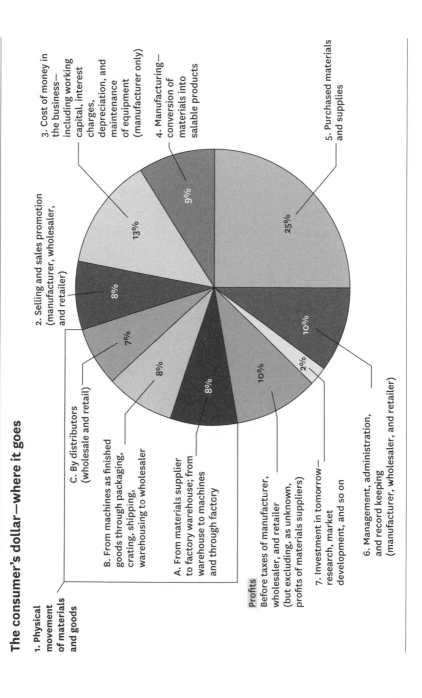

The consumer's dollar—where it goes

1. Physical movement of materials and goods

C. By distributors (wholesale and retail)

B. From machines as finished goods through packaging, crating, shipping, warehousing to wholesaler

A. From materials supplier to factory warehouse; from warehouse to machines and through factory

2. Selling and sales promotion (manufacturer, wholesaler, and retailer)

3. Cost of money in the business—including working capital, interest charges, depreciation, and maintenance of equipment (manufacturer only)

4. Manufacturing—conversion of materials into salable products

5. Purchased materials and supplies

6. Management, administration, and record keeping (manufacturer, wholesaler, and retailer)

7. Investment in tomorrow—research, market development, and so on

Profits
Before taxes of manufacturer, wholesaler, and retailer (but excluding, as unknown, profits of materials suppliers)

25%

10%

2%

10%

8%

8%

7%

8%

13%

9%

stream, and ignores the accountant's restriction that only those costs which are incurred *within* the legal entity of the business should be considered.

As to results, the important conclusions in this particular example are obvious: where most businesses concentrate their cost control efforts—i.e., on manufacturing—there is not much to be gained except by a real "breakthrough," such as a radically different process. The potentially most productive cost centers either lie *outside* the business, especially in distribution, and require very different treatment from the usual routine of "cost reduction," or they are areas that management rarely even "sees," such as the cost of money.

What Ought to Be

The next practical step is that of analyzing how resources are *now* being allocated to product lines, to staff support activities, and to cost centers. The analysis must, of course, be qualitative as well as quantitative. For numbers do not by themselves give the answers to questions like these:

- "Are advertising and promotion dollars going to the right products?"

- "Are capital equipment allocations in accord with realistic expectations for future demands that will be placed on the company?"

- "Is the company's allocation schedule supporting the best people and their activities?"

- "Are these good people deployed full-time on important jobs, or are they spread over so many assignments that they cannot do any one job properly?"

Answers to questions of this sort are often unpleasant, and the remedies they cry out for unpleasant to contemplate. Moving from the allocation stage to the decision stage, consequently, often takes courage.

Priority Decisions

There is only one rule that applies here. Specifically: *The areas of greatest potential for opportunity and results are to be given the fullest resource support—in quantity and quality—before the next promising area gets anything.*

Perhaps the area where the toughest and most risky decisions have to be made is that involving products, for the choices are seldom clear-cut and simple. For instance, products will often tend to group themselves into five groups—two with high-contribution potential, three with low- or minus-contribution potential, one in-between. What is fairly typical is a breakdown such as this:

- *Tomorrow's breadwinners*—new products or today's breadwinners modified and improved (rarely today's breadwinners unchanged).

- *Today's breadwinners*—the innovations of yesterday.

- *Products capable of becoming net contributors if something drastic is done;* e.g., converting a good many buyers of "special" variations of limited utility into customers for a new, massive "regular" line. (This is the in-between category.)

- *Yesterday's breadwinners*—typically products with high volume, but badly fragmented into "specials," small orders, and the like, and requiring such massive support as to eat up all they earn, and plenty more. Yet this is—next to the category following—the product class to which the largest and best resources are usually allocated. ("Defensive research" is a common example.)

- *The "also rans"*—typically the high hopes of yesterday that, while they did not work out well, nevertheless did not become outright failures. These are always minus contributors, and practically never become successes no matter how much is poured into them. Yet there is usually far too much managerial and technical ego involved in them to drop them.

- *The failures*—these rarely are a real problem as they tend to liquidate themselves.

This ranking suggests the line that decisions ought to follow. To begin with, the first category should be supplied the necessary resources—and usually a little more than seems necessary. Next, today's breadwinners ought to receive support. By then even a company rich in talent will have to begin to ration. Of the products capable of becoming major contributors, only those should be supported which have either the greatest probability of being reformed, successfully, or would make an *extraordinary* contribution if the reform were accomplished.

And from this point on there just are no high-potential resources available, as a rule—not even in the biggest, best-managed, and most profitable business. The lower half of the third group and groups four, five, and six, either have to produce without any resources and efforts or should be allowed to die. "Yesterday's breadwinner," for instance, often makes a respectable "milch cow" with high yields for a few more years. To expect more and to plow dollars into artificial respiration when the product finally begins to fade is just plain foolish.

The "also rans," who after four or five years of trial and hard work are still runts in the product litter and far below their original expectation, should always be abandoned. There is no greater drain on a business than the product that "almost made it." This is especially true if everyone in the company is convinced that, by quality, by design, or by the cost and difficulty of making it (that is what engineers usually mean when they say "quality"), the pet product is "entitled" to success.

This is part of the last and most crucial "how to do it" requirement: the courage to go through with logical decisions—despite all pleas to give this or that product another chance, and despite all such specious alibis as the accountant's "it absorbs overhead" or the sales manager's "we need a full product line." (Of course, these are not always unfounded alibis, but the burden of proof of every alibi rests with those that plead it.) It would be nice if I did, but unfortunately I know of no procedure or checklist for managerial courage.

Conclusion

What I have sketched out in this article is the manager's real work. As such it requires that he attack the problem of increasing business effectiveness systematically—with a plan of action, with a method of analysis, and with an understanding of the tools he needs.

And while the job to be done may look different in every individual company, one basic truth will always be present: every product and every activity of a business begins to obsolesce as soon as it is started. Every product, every operation, and every activity in a business should, therefore, be put on trial for its life every two or three years. Each should be considered the way we consider a proposal to go into a *new* product, a new operation or activity—complete with budget, capital appropriations request, and so on. One question should be asked of each: "If we were not in this already, would we now go into it?" And if the answer is "no," the next question should be: "How do we get out and how fast?"

The end products of the manager's work are decisions and actions, rather than knowledge and insight. The crucial decision is the allocation of efforts. And no matter how painful, one rule should be adhered to: *in allocating resources, especially human resources of high potential, the needs of those areas which offer great promise must first be satisfied to the fullest extent possible.* If this means that there are no truly productive resources left for a lot of things it would be nice, but not vital, to have or to do, then it is better—much better—to abandon these uses, and not to fritter away high-potential resources or attempt to get results with low-potential ones. This calls for painful decisions, and risky ones. But that, after all, is what managers are paid for.

Originally published in May–June 1963. Reprint 63303

Notes

1. This was brought out clearly by J. Roger Morrison and Richard F. Neuschel, "The Second Squeeze on Profits," HBR July–August 1962, p. 49; see also "Different Dollars," by Louis E. Newman and Sidney Brunell, in the same issue, p. 74.

2. See Morrison and Neuschel, op. cit.; and John Dearden, "Profit-Planning Accounting for Small Firms," HBR March–April 1963, p. 66.

The Effective
Decision

EFFECTIVE EXECUTIVES DO NOT MAKE a great many decisions. They concentrate on what is important. They try to make the few important decisions on the highest level of conceptual understanding. They try to find the constants in a situation, to think through what is strategic and generic rather than to "solve problems." They are, therefore, not overly impressed by speed in decision making; rather, they consider virtuosity in manipulating a great many variables a symptom of sloppy thinking. They want to know what the decision is all about and what the underlying realities are which it has to satisfy. They want impact rather than technique. And they want to be sound rather than clever.

Effective executives know when a decision has to be based on principle and when it should be made pragmatically, on the merits of the case. They know the trickiest decision is that between the right and the wrong compromise, and they have learned to tell one from the other. They know that the most time-consuming step in the process is not making the decision but putting it into effect. Unless a decision has degenerated into work, it is not a decision; it is at best a good intention. This means that, while the effective decision itself is based on the highest level of conceptual understanding, the action commitment should be as close as possible to the capacities of the people who have to carry it out. Above all, effective executives know that decision making has its own systematic process and its own clearly defined elements.

Sequential Steps

The elements do not by themselves "make" the decisions. Indeed, every decision is a risk-taking judgment. But unless these elements are the stepping stones of the decision process, the executive will not arrive at a right, and certainly not at an effective, decision. Therefore, in this article I shall describe the sequence of steps involved in the decision-making process.

1. *Classifying the problem.* Is it generic? Is it exceptional and unique? Or is it the first manifestation of a new genus for which a rule has yet to be developed?

2. *Defining the problem.* What are we dealing with?

3. *Specifying the answer to the problem.* What are the "boundary conditions"?

4. *Deciding what is "right," rather than what is acceptable, in order to meet the boundary conditions.* What will fully satisfy the specifications *before* attention is given to the compromises, adaptations, and concessions needed to make the decision acceptable?

5. *Building into the decision the action to carry it out.* What does the action commitment have to be? Who has to know about it?

6. *Testing the validity and effectiveness of the decision against the actual course of events.* How is the decision being carried out? Are the assumptions on which it is based appropriate or obsolete?

Let us take a look at each of these individual elements.

The Classification

The effective decision maker asks: Is this a symptom of a fundamental disorder or a stray event? The generic always has to be answered through a rule, a principle. But the truly exceptional event can only be handled as such and as it comes.

Idea in Brief

Effective decision making requires a distinct sequence of steps. The sequence includes identifying a generic or unique problem, defining the issues of the problem, determining the required specifications, deciding what is right rather than what is acceptable, building action into the decision, and using feedback which tests the validity.

Strictly speaking, the executive might distinguish among four, rather than between two, different types of occurrences.

First, there is the truly generic event, of which the individual occurrence is only a symptom. Most of the "problems" that come up in the course of the executive's work are of this nature. Inventory decisions in a business, for instance, are not "decisions." They are adaptations. The problem is generic. This is even more likely to be true of occurrences within manufacturing organizations. For example:

A product control and engineering group will typically handle many hundreds of problems in the course of a month. Yet, whenever these are analyzed, the great majority prove to be just symptoms—and manifestations—of underlying basic situations. The individual process control engineer or production engineer who works in one part of the plant usually cannot see this. He might have a few problems each month with the couplings in the pipes that carry steam or hot liquids, and that's all.

Only when the total workload of the group over several months is analyzed does the generic problem appear. Then it is seen that temperatures or pressures have become too great for the existing equipment and that the couplings holding the various lines together need to be redesigned for greater loads. Until this analysis is done, process control will spend a tremendous amount of time fixing leaks without ever getting control of the situation.

The second type of occurrence is the problem which, while a unique event for the individual institution, is actually generic. Consider:

The company that receives an offer to merge from another, larger one, will never receive such an offer again if it accepts. This is a nonrecurrent situation as far as the individual company, its board of directors, and its management are concerned. But it is, of course, a generic situation which occurs all the time. Thinking through whether to accept or to reject the offer requires some general rules. For these, however, the executive has to look to the experience of others.

Next there is the truly exceptional event that the executive must distinguish. To illustrate:

The huge power failure that plunged into darkness the whole of Northeastern North America from St. Lawrence to Washington in November 1965 was, according to first explanations, a truly exceptional situation. So was the thalidomide tragedy which led to the birth of so many deformed babies in the early 1960s. The probability of either of these events occurring, we were told, was one in ten million or one in a hundred million, and concatenations of these events were as unlikely ever to recur again as it is unlikely, for instance, for the chair on which I sit to disintegrate into its constituent atoms.

Truly unique events are rare, however. Whenever one appears, the decision maker has to ask: Is this a true exception or only the first manifestation of a new genus? And this—the early manifestation of a new generic problem—is the fourth and last category of events with which the decision process deals. Thus:

We know now that both the Northeastern power failure and the thalidomide tragedy were only the first occurrences of what, under conditions of modern power technology or of modern pharmacology, are likely to become fairly frequent occurrences unless generic solutions are found.

All events but the truly unique require a generic solution. They require a rule, a policy, or a principle. Once the right principle has been developed, all manifestations of the same generic situation can be handled pragmatically—that is, by adaptation of the rule to the concrete circumstances of the case. Truly unique events, however, must be treated individually. The executive cannot develop rules for the exceptional.

The effective decision maker spends time determining which of the four different situations is happening. The wrong decision will be made if the situation is classified incorrectly.

By far the most common mistake of the decision maker is to treat a generic situation as if it were a series of unique events—that is, to be pragmatic when lacking the generic understanding and principle. The inevitable result is frustration and futility. This was clearly shown, I think, by the failure of most of the policies, both domestic and foreign, of the Kennedy Administration. Consider:

> For all the brilliance of its members, the Administration achieved fundamentally only one success, and that was in the Cuban missile crisis. Otherwise, it achieved practically nothing. The main reason was surely what its members called "pragmatism"— namely, the Administration's refusal to develop rules and principles, and its insistence on training everything "on its merits." Yet it was clear to everyone, including the members of the Administration, that the basic assumptions on which its policies rested—the valid assumptions of the immediate postwar years—had become increasingly unrealistic in international, as well as in domestic, affairs in the 1960's.

Equally common is the mistake of treating a new event as if it were just another example of the old problem to which, therefore, the old rules should be applied:

> This was the error that snowballed the local power failure on the New York–Ontario border into the great Northeastern blackout. The power engineers, especially in New York City, applied the

right rule for a normal overload. Yet their own instruments had signaled that something quite extraordinary was going on which called for exceptional, rather than standard, countermeasures.

By contrast, the one great triumph of President Kennedy in the Cuban missile crisis rested on acceptance of the challenge to think through an extraordinary, exceptional occurrence. As soon as he accepted this, his own tremendous resources of intelligence and courage effectively came into play.

The Definition

Once a problem has been classified as generic or unique, it is usually fairly easy to define. "What is this all about?" "What is pertinent here?" "What is the key to this situation?" Questions such as these are familiar. But only the truly effective decision makers are aware that the danger in this step is not the wrong definition; it is the plausible but incomplete one. For example:

The American automobile industry held to a plausible but incomplete definition of the problem of automotive safety. It was this lack of awareness—far more than any reluctance to spend money on safety engineering—that eventually, in 1966, brought the industry under sudden and sharp Congressional attack for its unsafe cars and then left the industry totally bewildered by the attack. It simply is not true that the industry has paid scant attention to safety.

On the contrary, it has worked hard at safer highway engineering and at driver training, believing these to be the major areas for concern. That accidents are caused by unsafe roads and unsafe drivers is plausible enough. Indeed, all other agencies concerned with automotive safety, from the highway police to the high schools, picked the same targets for their campaigns. These campaigns have produced results. The number of accidents on highways built for safety has been greatly lessened. Similarly, safety-trained drivers have been involved in far fewer accidents.

But although the ratio of accidents per thousand cars or per thousand miles driven has been going down, the total number of accidents and the severity of them have kept creeping up. It should therefore have become clear long ago that something would have to be done about the small but significant probability that accidents will occur despite safety laws and safety training.

This means that future safety campaigns will have to be supplemented by engineering to make accidents themselves less dangerous. Whereas cars have been engineered to be safe when used correctly, they will also have to be engineered for safety when used incorrectly.

There is only one safeguard against becoming the prisoner of an incomplete definition: check it again and again against *all* the observable facts, and throw out a definition the moment it fails to encompass any of them.

Effective decision makers always test for signs that something is atypical or something unusual is happening, always asking: Does the definition explain the observed events, and does it explain all of them? They always write out what the definition is expected to make happen—for instance, make automobile accidents disappear—and then test regularly to see if this really happens. Finally, they go back and think the problem through again whenever they see something atypical, when they find unexplained phenomena, or when the course of events deviates, even in details, from expectations.

These are in essence the rules Hippocrates laid down for medical diagnosis well over 2,000 years ago. They are the rules for scientific observation first formulated by Aristotle and then reaffirmed by Galileo 300 years ago. These, in other words, are old, well-known, time-tested rules, which an executive can learn and apply systematically.

The Specifications

The next major element in the decision process is defining clear specifications as to what the decision has to accomplish. What are the objectives the decision has to reach? What are the minimum goals it has to attain? What are the conditions it has to satisfy? In science these are known as "boundary condi-tions." A decision, to be effective, needs to satisfy the boundary conditions. Consider:

"Can our needs be satisfied," Alfred P. Sloan, Jr. presumably asked himself when he took command of General Motors in 1922, "by removing the autonomy of our division heads?" His answer was clearly in the negative. The boundary conditions of his problem demanded strength and responsibility in the chief operating positions. This was needed as much as unity and control at the center. Everyone before Sloan had seen the problem as one of personalities—to be solved through a struggle for power from which one man would emerge victorious. The boundary conditions, Sloan realized, demanded a solution to a constitutional problem—to be solved through a new structure: decentralization which balanced local autonomy of operations with central control of direction and policy.

A decision that does not satisfy the boundary conditions is worse than one which wrongly defines the problem. It is all but impossible to salvage the decision that starts with the right premises but stops short of the right conclusions. Furthermore, clear thinking about the boundary conditions is needed to know when a decision has to be abandoned. The most common cause of failure in a decision lies not in its being wrong initially. Rather, it is a subsequent shift in the goals—the specifications—which makes the prior right decision suddenly inappropriate. And unless the decision maker has kept the boundary conditions clear, so as to make possible the immediate replacement of the outflanked decision with a new and appropriate policy, he may not even notice that things have changed. For example:

> Franklin D. Roosevelt was bitterly attacked for his switch from conservative candidate in 1932 to radical president in 1933. But it wasn't Roosevelt who changed. The sudden economic collapse which occurred between the summer of 1932 and the spring of 1933 changed the specifications. A policy appropriate to the goal of national economic recovery—which a conservative economic policy might have been—was no longer appropriate when, with the Bank Holiday, the goal had to become political and social

cohesion. When the boundary conditions changed, Roosevelt immediately substituted a political objective (reform) for his former economic one (recovery).

Above all, clear thinking about the boundary conditions is needed to identify the most dangerous of all possible decisions: the one in which the specifications that have to be satisfied are essentially incompatible. In other words, this is the decision that might—just might—work if nothing whatever goes wrong. A classic case is President Kennedy's Bay of Pigs decision:

One specification was clearly Castro's overthrow. The other was to make it appear that the invasion was a "spontaneous" uprising of the Cubans. But these two specifications would have been compatible with each other only if an immediate island-wide uprising against Castro would have completely paralyzed the Cuban army. And while this was not impossible, it clearly was not probable in such a tightly controlled police state.

Decisions of this sort are usually called "gambles." But actually they arise from something much less rational than a gamble— namely, a hope against hope that two (or more) clearly incompatible specifications can be fulfilled simultaneously. This is hoping for a miracle; and the trouble with miracles is not that they happen so rarely, but that they are, alas, singularly unreliable.

Everyone can make the wrong decision. In fact, everyone will sometimes make a wrong decision. But no executive needs to make a decision which, on the face of it, seems to make sense but, in reality, falls short of satisfying the boundary conditions.

The Decision

The effective executive has to start out with what is "right" rather than what is acceptable precisely because a compromise is always necessary in the end. But if what will satisfy the boundary conditions is not known, the decision maker cannot distinguish between the right compromise and the wrong compromise—and may end up by making the wrong compromise. Consider:

I was taught this lesson in 1944 when I started on my first big consulting assignment. It was a study of the management structure and policies of General Motors Corporation. Alfred P. Sloan, Jr., who was then chairman and chief executive officer of the company, called me to his office at the start of my assignment and said: "I shall not tell you what to study, what to write, or what conclusions to come to. This is your task. My only instruction to you is to put down what you think is right as you see it. Don't you worry about our reaction. Don't you worry about whether we will like this or dislike that. And don't you, above all, concern yourself with the compromises that might be needed to make your conclusions acceptable. There is not one executive in this company who does not know how to make every single conceivable compromise without any help from you. But he can't make the right compromise unless you first tell him what *right* is."

The effective executive knows that there are two different kinds of compromise. One is expressed in the old proverb, "Half a loaf is better than no bread." The other, in the story of the judgment of Solomon, is clearly based on the realization that "half a baby is worse than no baby at all." In the first instance, the boundary conditions are still being satisfied. The purpose of bread is to provide food, and half a loaf is still food. Half a baby, however, does not satisfy the boundary conditions. For half a baby is not half of a living and growing child.

It is a waste of time to worry about what will be acceptable and what the decision maker should or should not say so as not to evoke resistance. (The things one worries about seldom happen, while objections and difficulties no one thought about may suddenly turn out to be almost insurmountable obstacles.) In other words, the decision maker gains nothing by starting out with the question, "What is acceptable?" For in the process of answering it, he or she usually gives away the important things and loses any chance to come up with an effective—let alone the right—answer.

The Action

Converting the decision into action is the fifth major element in the decision process. While thinking through the boundary conditions is the most difficult step in decision making, converting the decision into effective action is usually the most time-consuming one. Yet a decision will not become effective unless the action commitments have been built into it from the start. In fact, no decision has been made unless carrying it out in specific steps has become someone's work assignment and responsibility. Until then, it is only a good intention.

The flaw in so many policy statements, especially those of business, is that they contain no action commitment—to carry them out is no one's specific work and responsibility. Small wonder then that the people in the organization tend to view such statements cynically, if not as declarations of what top management is really *not* going to do.

Converting a decision into action requires answering several distinct questions: Who has to know of this decision? What action has to be taken? Who is to take it? What does the action have to be so that the people who have to do it *can* do it? The first and the last of these questions are too often overlooked—with dire results. A story that has become a legend among operations researchers illustrates the importance of the question, "Who has to know?":

A major manufacturer of industrial equipment decided several years ago to discontinue one of its models that had for years been standard equipment on a line of machine tools, many of which were still in use. It was, therefore, decided to sell the model to present owners of the old equipment for another three years as a replacement, and then to stop making and selling it. Orders for this particular model had been going down for a good many years. But they shot up immediately as customers reordered against the day when the model would no longer be available. No one had, however, asked, "Who needs to know of this decision?"

Consequently, nobody informed the purchasing clerk who was in charge of buying the parts from which the model itself was being assembled. His instructions were to buy parts in a given ratio to current sales—and the instructions remained unchanged.

Thus, when the time came to discontinue further production of the model, the company had in its warehouse enough parts for another 8 to 10 years of production, parts that had to be written off at a considerable loss.

The action must also be appropriate to the capacities of the people who have to carry it out. Thus:

A large U.S. chemical company found itself, in recent years, with fairly large amounts of blocked currency in two West African countries. To protect this money, top management decided to invest it locally in businesses which would: (1) contribute to the local economy, (2) not require imports from abroad, and (3) if successful, be the kind that could be sold to local investors if and when currency remittances became possible again. To establish these businesses, the company developed a simple chemical process to preserve a tropical fruit—a staple crop in both countries—which, up until then, had suffered serious spoilage in transit to its Western markets.

The business was a success in both countries. But in one country the local manager set the business up in such a manner that it required highly skilled and technically trained management of a kind not easily available in West Africa. In the other country, the local manager thought through the capacities of the people who would eventually have to run the business. Consequently, he worked hard at making both the process and the business simple, and at staffing his operation from the start with local nationals right up to the top management level.

A few years later it became possible again to transfer currency from these two countries. But, though the business flourished, no buyer could be found for it in the first country. No one available locally had the necessary managerial and technical skills to run it, and so the business had to be liquidated at a loss. In the other country, so many local entrepreneurs were eager to buy the business that the company repatriated its original investment with a substantial profit.

The chemical process and the business built on it were essentially the same in both places. But in the first country no one had asked, "What kind of people do we have available to make this decision effective? And what can they do?" As a result, the decision itself became frustrated.

This action commitment becomes doubly important when people have to change their behavior, habits, or attitudes if a decision is to become effective. Here, the executive must make sure not only that the responsibility for the action is clearly assigned, but that the people assigned are capable of carrying it out. Thus the decision maker has to make sure that the measurements, the standards for accomplishment, and the incentives of those charged with the action responsibility are changed simultaneously. Otherwise, the organization people will get caught in a paralyzing internal emotional conflict. Consider these two examples:

- When Theodore Vail was president of the Bell Telephone System 60 years ago, he decided that its business was service. This decision explains in large part why the United States (and Canada) has today an investor-owned, rather than a nationalized, telephone system. Yet this policy statement might have remained a dead letter if Vail had not at the same time designed yardsticks of service performance and introduced these as a means to measure, and ultimately to reward, managerial performance. The Bell managers of that time were used to being measured by the profitability (or at least by the cost) of their units. The new yardsticks resulted in the rapid acceptance of the new objectives.

- In sharp contrast is the recent failure of a brilliant chairman and chief executive to make effective a new organization structure and new objectives in an old, large, and proud U.S. company. Everyone agreed that the changes were needed. The company, after many years as leader of its industry, showed definite signs of aging. In many markets newer, smaller, and more aggressive competitors were outflanking it. But contrary to the action required to gain acceptance for the new ideas, the chairman—in order to placate the opposition—promoted prominent spokesmen of the old school into the most visible and highest salaried positions—in particular into three new executive vice presidencies. This meant only one thing to the people in the company: "They don't really mean it." If the greatest rewards are given for behavior contrary to that which the new course of action requires, then everyone will conclude that this is what the people at the top really want and are going to reward.

Only the most effective executive can do what Vail did—build the execution of his decision into the decision itself. But every executive can think through what action commitments a specific decision requires, what work assignments follow from it, and what people are available to carry it out.

The Feedback

Finally, information monitoring and reporting have to be built into the decision to provide continuous testing, against actual events, of the expectations that underlie the decisions. Decisions are made by people. People are fallible; at best, their works do not last long. Even the best decision has a high probability of being wrong. Even the most effective one eventually becomes obsolete.

This surely needs no documentation. And every executive always builds organized feedback—reports, figures, studies—into his or her decision to monitor and report on it. Yet far too many decisions fail to achieve their anticipated results, or indeed ever to become effective, despite all these feedback reports. Just as the view from the Matterhorn cannot be visualized by studying a map of Switzerland (one abstraction), a decision cannot be fully and accurately evaluated by studying a report. That is because reports are, of necessity, abstractions.

Effective decision makers know this and follow a rule which the military developed long ago. The commander who makes a decision does not depend on reports to see how it is being carried out. The commander or an aide goes and looks. The reason is not that effective decision makers (or effective commanders) distrust their subordinates. Rather, they learned the hard way to distrust abstract "communications."

With the coming of the computer this feedback element will become even more important, for the decision maker will in all likelihood be even further removed from the scene of action. Unless he or she accepts, as a matter of course, that he or she had better go out and look at the scene of action, he or she will be increasingly divorced from reality. All a computer can handle is abstractions. And abstractions can be relied on only if they are constantly checked against concrete results. Otherwise, they are certain to mislead.

To go and look is also the best, if not the only way, for an executive to test whether the assumptions on which the decision has been made are still valid or whether they are becoming obsolete and need to be thought through again. And the executive always has to expect the assumptions to become obsolete sooner or later. Reality never stands still very long.

Failure to go out and look is the typical reason for persisting in a course of action long after it has ceased to be appropriate or even rational. This is true for business decisions as well as for governmental policies. It explains in large measure the failure of Stalin's cold war policy in Europe, but also the inability of the United States to adjust its policies to the realities of a Europe restored to prosperity and economic growth, and the failure of the British to accept, until too late, the reality of the European Common Market. Moreover, in any business I know, failure to go out and look at customers and markets, at competitors and their products, is also a major reason for poor, ineffectual, and wrong decisions.

Decision makers need organized information for feedback. They need reports and figures. But unless they build their feedback around direct exposure to reality—unless they discipline themselves to go out and look—they condemn themselves to a sterile dogmatism.

Concluding Note

Decision making is only one of the tasks of an executive. It usually takes but a small fraction of his or her time. But to make the important decisions is the *specific* executive task. Only an executive makes such decisions.

An *effective* executive makes these decisions as a systematic process with clearly defined elements and in a distinct sequence of steps. Indeed, to be expected (by virtue of position or knowledge) to make decisions that have significant and positive impact on the entire organization, its performance, and its results characterizes the effective executive.

Originally published in January–February 1967. Reprint 67105

How to Make People Decisions

EXECUTIVES SPEND MORE TIME on managing people and making people decisions than on anything else—and they should. No other decisions are so long lasting in their consequences or so difficult to unmake. And yet, by and large, executives make poor promotion and staffing decisions. By all accounts, their batting average is no better than .333: at most one-third of such decisions turn out right; one-third are minimally effective; and one-third are outright failures.

In no other area of management would we put up with such miserable performance. Indeed, we need not and should not. Managers making people decisions will never be perfect, of course, but they should come pretty close to batting 1,000—especially since in no other area of management do we know as much.

Some executives' people decisions have, however, approached perfection. At the time of Pearl Harbor, every single general officer in the U.S. Army was overage. Although none of the younger men had been tested in combat or in a significant troup command, the United States came out of World War II with the largest corps of competent general officers any army has ever had. George C. Marshall, the army's chief of staff, had personally chosen each man. Not all were great successes, but practically none were outright failures.

In the 40 or so years during which he ran General Motors, Alfred P. Sloan, Jr. picked every GM executive—down to the manufacturing managers, controllers, engineering managers, and master mechanics at even the smallest accessory division. By today's standards, Sloan's vision and values may seem narrow. They were. He was concerned only with performance in and for GM. Nonetheless, his long-term performance in placing people in the right jobs was flawless.

The Basic Principles

There is no such thing as an infallible judge of people, at least not on this side of the Pearly Gates. There are, however, a few executives who take their people decisions seriously and work at them.

Marshall and Sloan were about as different as two human beings can be, but they followed, and quite consciously, much the same principles in making people decisions:

- If I put a person into a job and he or she does not perform, I have made a mistake. I have no business blaming that person, no business invoking the "Peter Principle," no business complaining. I have made a mistake.

- "The soldier has a right to competent command" was already an old maxim at the time of Julius Caesar. It is the duty of managers to make sure that the responsible people in their organizations perform.

- Of all the decisions an executive makes, none are as important as the decisions about people because they determine the performance capacity of the organization. Therefore, I'd better make these decisions well.

- The one "don't": do not give new people new major assignments, for doing so only compounds the risks. Give this sort of assignment to someone whose behavior and habits you know and who has earned trust and credibility within your organization. Put a high-level newcomer first into an established position where the expectations are known and help is available.

Idea in Brief

People decisions are long lasting in their consequences and difficult to unmake. At most one third of such decisions come out right. Executives who take their people decisions seriously will find the following principles helpful: (1) take responsibility for the decision—if the person the executive places in a position does not perform, the executive has made a mistake; (2) it is the duty of managers to make sure that the responsible persons in their organizations perform; (3) make the decision well; (4) don't give new people major new assignments. There are also some basic steps managers can follow in making effective promotion and staffing decisions.

Some of the worst staffing failures I have seen involved brilliant Europeans hired by U.S. companies—one based in Pittsburgh; the other, Chicago—to head up new European ventures. Dr. Hans Schmidt and M. Jean Perrin (only the names are fictitious) were hailed as geniuses when they came in. A year later they were both out, totally defeated.

No one in Pittsburgh had understood that Schmidt's training and temperament would make him sit on a new assignment for the first six or nine months, thinking, studying, planning, getting ready for decisive action. Schmidt, in turn, had never even imagined that Pittsburgh expected instant action and immediate results. No one in Chicago had known that Perrin, while a solid and doggedly purposeful man, was excitable and mercurial, flailing his arms, making speeches about trivia, and sending up one trial balloon after another. Although both men subsequently became highly successful CEOs of major European corporations, both executives were failures in companies that did not know and understand them.

Two other U.S. companies successfully established businesses for the first time in Europe during the same period (the late 1960s and early 1970s). To initiate their projects, each sent to Europe a U.S. executive who had never before worked or lived there but whom people in the head offices knew thoroughly and understood well. In turn the two managers were thoroughly familiar with their companies. At the same time, each organization hired half a dozen young Europeans and placed them in upper-middle executive jobs in the United States. Within a few years, both companies had a solid European business and a trained, seasoned, and trusted corps of executives to run it.

As Winston Churchill's ancestor, the great Duke of Marlborough, observed some three centuries ago, "The basic trouble in coalition warfare is that one has to entrust victory if not one's life, to a fellow commander whom one knows by reputation rather than by performance."

In the corporation as in the military, without personal knowledge built up over a period of time there can be neither trust nor effective communication.

The Decision Steps

Just as there are only a few basic principles, there are only a few important steps to follow in making effective promotion and staffing decisions:

1. Think through the assignment

Job descriptions may last a long time. In one large manufacturing company, for example, the job description for the position of division general manager has hardly changed since the company began to decentralize 30 years ago. Indeed, the job description for bishops in the Roman Catholic church has not changed at all since canon law was first codified in the thirteenth century. But assignments change all the time, and unpredictably.

Once in the early 1940s, I told Alfred Sloan that he seemed to spend an inordinate amount of time pondering the assignment of a fairly low-level job—general sales manager of a small accessory division—before choosing among three equally qualified candidates. "Look at the assignment the last few times we had to fill the same job," Sloan answered. To my surprise, I found that the terms of the assignment were quite different on each occasion.

When putting a man in as division commander during World War II, George Marshall always looked first at the nature of the assignment for the next eighteen months or two years. To raise a division and train it is one assignment. To lead it in combat is quite another. To take command of a division that has been badly mauled and restore its morale and fighting strength is another still.

When the task is to select a new regional sales manager, the responsible executive must first know what the heart of the assignment is: to recruit and train new salespeople because, say, the present sales force is nearing retirement age? Or is it to open up new markets because the company's products, though doing well with old-line industries in the region, have not been able to penetrate new and growing markets? Or, since the bulk of sales still comes from products that are 25 years old, is it to establish a market presence for the company's new products? Each of these is a different assignment and requires a different kind of person.

2. Look at a number of potentially qualified people
The controlling word here is "number." Formal qualifications are a minimum for consideration; their absence disqualifies the candidate automatically. Equally important, the person and the assignment need to fit each other. To make an effective decision, an executive should look at three to five qualified candidates.

3. Think hard about how to look at these candidates
If an executive has studied the assignment, he or she understands what a new person would need to do with high priority and concentrated effort. The central question is not "What can this or that candidate do or not do?" It is, rather, "What are the strengths each possesses and are these the right strengths for the assignment?" Weaknesses are limitations, which may, of course, rule a candidate out. For instance, a person may be excellently qualified for the technical aspects of a job; but if the assignment requires above all the ability to build a team and this ability is lacking, then the fit is not right.

But effective executives do not start out by looking at weaknesses. You cannot build performance on weaknesses. You can build only on strengths. Both Marshall and Sloan were highly demanding men, but both knew that what matters is the ability to do the assignment.

If that exists, the company can always supply the rest. If it does not exist, the rest is useless.

If, for instance, a division needed an officer for a training assignment, Marshall looked for people who could turn recruits into soldiers. Every man that was good at this task usually had serious weaknesses in other areas. One was not particularly effective as a tactical commander and was positively hopeless when it came to strategy. Another had foot-in-mouth disease and got into trouble with the press. A third was vain, arrogant, egotistical, and fought constantly with his commanding officer. Never mind, could he train recruits? If the answer was yes—and especially if the answer was "he's the best"—he got the job.

In picking the members of their cabinets, Franklin Roosevelt and Harry Truman said, in effect: "Never mind personal weaknesses. Tell me first what each of them can do." It may not be coincidence that these two presidents had the strongest cabinets in twentieth-century U.S. history.

4. Discuss each of the candidates with several people who have worked with them

One executive's judgment alone is worthless. Because all of us have first impressions, prejudices, likes, and dislikes, we need to listen to what other people think. When the military picks general officers or the Catholic church picks bishops, this kind of extensive discussion is a formal step in their selection process. Competent executives do it informally. Hermann Abs, the former head of Deutsche Bank, picked more successful chief executives in recent times than anyone else. He personally chose most of the top-level managers who pulled off the postwar German "economic miracle," and he checked out each of them first with three or four of the person's former bosses or colleagues.

5. Make sure the appointee understands the job

After the appointee has been in a new job for three or four months, he or she should be focusing on the demands of that job rather than on the requirements of preceeding assignments. It is the executive's responsibility to call that person in and say, "You have now been regional sales manager—or whatever—for three months. What do you have to do to be a success in your new job? Think it through and come back in a week or ten days and show me in writing. But I can tell you one thing right away: the things you did to get the promotion are almost certainly the wrong things to do now."

If you do not follow this step, don't blame the candidate for poor performance. Blame yourself. You have failed in your duty as a manager.

The largest single source of failed promotions—and I know of no greater waste in U.S. management—is the failure to think through, and help others think through, what a new job requires. All too typical is the brilliant former student of mine who telephoned me a few months ago, almost in tears. "I got my first big chance a year ago," he said. "My company made me engineering manager. Now they tell me that I'm through. And yet I've done a better job than ever before. I have actually designed three successful new products for which we'll get patents."

It is only human to say to ourselves, "I must have done something right or I would not have gotten the big new job. Therefore, I had better do more of what I did to get the promotion now that I have it." It is not intuitively obvious to most people that a new and different job requires new and different behavior. Almost 50 years ago, a boss of mine challenged me four months after he had advanced me to a far more responsible position. Until he called me in, I had continued to do what I had done before. To his credit, he understood that it was his responsibility to make me see that a new job means different behavior, a different focus, and different relationships.

The High-Risk Decisions

Even if executives follow all these steps, some of their people decisions will still fail. These are, for the most part, the high-risk decisions that nevertheless have to be taken.

There is, for example, high risk in picking managers in professional organizations—for a research lab, say, or an engineering or corporate legal department. Professionals do not readily accept as their boss someone whose credentials in the field they do not respect. In choosing a manager of engineering, the choices are therefore limited to the top-flight engineers in the department. Yet there is no correlation (unless it be a negative one) between performance as a bench engineer and performance as a manager. Much the same is true when a high-performing operating manager gets a promotion to a staff job in headquarters or a staff expert moves into a line position. Temperamentally, operating people are frequently unsuited to the tensions, frustrations, and relationships of staff work, and vice versa. The first-rate regional sales manager may well become totally ineffective if promoted into market research, sales forecasting, or pricing.

We do not know how to test or predict whether a person's temperament will suit a new environment. We can find this out only by experience. If a move from one kind of work to another does not pan out, the executive who made the decision has to remove the misfit, and fast. But that executive also has to say, "I made a mistake, and it is my job to correct it." To keep misfits in a job they cannot do is not being kind; it is being cruel. But there is also no reason to let the person go. A company can always use a good bench engineer, a good analyst, a good sales manager. The proper course of action—and it works most times—is to offer the misfit a return to the old job or an equivalent.

People decisions may also fail because a job has become what New England ship captains 150 years ago called a "widow maker." When a clipper ship, no matter how well designed and constructed, began to have fatal "accidents," the owners did not redesign or rebuild the ship. They broke it up as fast as possible.

Widow makers—that is, jobs that regularly defeat even good people—appear most often when a company grows or changes fast. For instance, in the 1960s and early 1970s, the job of "international vice president" in U.S. banks became a widow maker. It had always been an easy job to fill. In fact, it had long been considered a job in which banks could safely put "also rans" and could expect them to perform well. Then, suddenly, the job began to defeat one new incumbent after another. What had happened, as hindsight now tells us, is that international activity quickly and without warning became an integral part of the daily business of major banks and their corporate customers. What had been until then an easy job became, literally, a "nonjob" that nobody could do.

Whenever a job defeats two people in a row, who in their earlier assignments had performed well, a company has a widow maker on its hands. When this happens, a responsible executive should not ask the headhunter for a universal genius. Instead abolish the job. Any job that ordinarily competent people cannot perform is a job that cannot be staffed. Unless changed, it will predictably defeat the third incumbent the way it defeated the first two.

Making the right people decisions is the ultimate means of controlling an organization well. Such decisions reveal how competent management is, what its values are, and whether it takes its job seriously. No matter how hard managers try to keep their decisions a secret—and some still try hard—people decisions cannot be hidden. They are eminently visible.

Executives often cannot judge whether a strategic move is a wise one. Nor are they necessarily interested. "I don't know why we are buying this business in Australia, but it won't interfere with what we are doing here in Fort Worth" is a common reaction. But when the same executives read that "Joe Smith has been made controller in the XYZ division," they usually know Joe much better than top management does. These executives should be able to say, "Joe deserves the promotion; he is an excellent choice—just the person that division needs to get the controls appropriate for its rapid growth."

If, however, Joe got promoted because he is a politician, everybody will know it. They will all say to themselves, "Okay, that is the way to get ahead in this company." They will despise their management for forcing them to become politicians but will either quit or become politicians themselves in the end. As we have known for a long time, people in organizations tend to behave as they see others being rewarded. And when the rewards go to nonperformance, to flattery, or to mere cleverness, the organization will soon decline into nonperformance, flattery, or cleverness.

Executives who do not make the effort to get their people decisions right do more than risk poor performance. They risk losing their organization's respect.

Originally published in July–August 1985. Reprint 85406

They're Not Employees, They're People

TWO EXTRAORDINARY CHANGES have crept up on the business world without most of us paying much attention to them. First, a staggering number of people who work for organizations are no longer traditional employees of those organizations. And second, a growing number of businesses have outsourced employee relations; they no longer manage major aspects of their relationships with the people who *are* their formal employees. These trends are unlikely to reverse themselves anytime soon. In fact, they'll probably accelerate. And they're happening for some very good reasons, as we'll see.

That said, the attenuation of the relationship between people and the organizations they work for represents a grave danger to business. It's one thing for a company to take advantage of long-term freelance talent or to outsource the more tedious aspects of its human resources management. It's quite another to forget, in the process, that developing talent is business's most important task—the sine qua non of competition in a knowledge economy. If by off-loading employee relations, organizations also lose their capacity to develop people, they will have made a devil's bargain indeed.

Every working day, one of the world's biggest private employers, the Swiss company Adecco, places nearly 700,000 temporary and full-time clerical, industrial, and technical associates with businesses all over the world—perhaps as many as 250,000 workers in the United States. Adecco is the temp industry giant, but it has only a small share of a totally splintered global market. In the United States alone, there are thousands of such companies that together place some 2.5 million workers each day. Worldwide, at least 8 million, if not 10 million, temp workers are placed each day. And 70% of all temps work full time.

When the temp industry first started nearly 50 years ago, it supplied low-level clerks to take the place of ledger keepers, receptionists, telephone operators, stenographers, or the ladies in the typing pool who were sick or on vacation. Today there are temp suppliers for every kind of job, all the way up to CEO. One company, for instance, supplies manufacturing managers who can lead new plants from their inception until the facilities are in full production. Another supplies highly skilled health care professionals such as nurse anesthesiologists.

In a related but distinct development, the *professional employee organization* (PEO) was the fastest-growing business service in the United States during the 1990s. These businesses manage their clients' employees as well as their clients' employee relations—that is, the administrative, HR kinds of tasks associated with managing those employees. PEOs were virtually unknown only ten years ago but by 2000 had become the "coemployers" of 2.5 million to 3 million blue-collar and white-collar U.S. workers. There are now at least 1,800 such organizations; they even have their own trade association and their own monthly journal.

PEOs, like temp agencies, have vastly expanded their scope in recent years. The first PEOs in the late 1980s offered to do bookkeeping, especially payroll, for their clients. Now PEOs can take care of almost every task in employee management and relations: record keeping and legal compliance; hiring, training, placements, promotions, firings, and layoffs; and retirement plans and pen-

Idea in Brief

In this essay, Peter Drucker examines the changing dynamics of the workforce—in particular, the need for organizations to take just as much care and responsibility when managing temporary and contract workers as they do with their traditional employees.

Two fast-growing trends are demanding that business leaders pay more attention to employee relations, Drucker says. First is the rise of the temporary, or contract, worker; 8 million to 10 million temp workers are placed each day worldwide. And they're not just filling in at reception desks. Today, there are temp suppliers for every kind of job, all the way up to CEO. Second, a growing number of businesses are outsourcing their employee relations to professional employee organizations (PEOs)—third-party groups that handle

the ever-mounting administrative tasks associated with managing a company's employees. (Managers can easily spend up to one-quarter of their time on employee-related rules, regulations, and paperwork.) Driving these trends, Drucker observes, is the shift from a dependency on manual labor to create wealth and jobs to a dependency on specialization and knowledge. Leaders are increasingly trying to keep up with the needs of many small groups of product or service experts within their companies.

Temps and PEOs free up leaders to focus on the business rather than on HR files and paperwork. But if organizations outsource those functions, they need to be careful not to damage relationships with their people in the process, Drucker concludes.

sion payments. PEOs originally confined themselves to taking care of employee relations at small businesses. But Exult, probably the best known PEO, was designed from the start to be the coemployer for global *Fortune* 500 companies. It numbers among its clients BP Amoco, Unisys, and Tenneco Automotive. Founded just four years ago, it has already gone public and is traded on the Nasdaq. Another PEO, designed originally to handle payroll functions for businesses with fewer than 20 employees, is about to take on managing the 120,000 employees of one of the largest U.S. states.

Both the temp industry and the PEOs are growing quickly. Adecco is expanding at a rate of 15% a year. In the second quarter of 2001, Exult's revenue grew 48%, from $43.5 million to $64.3 million. And the PEO industry as a whole is growing at a rate of 30% a year. Collectively, PEOs expect to be the coemployers of 10 million U.S. workers by 2005.

The reader may wonder, How can a manager function if she's not in charge of hiring, promoting, or firing the people in her department? I posed this question to a senior executive at BP Amoco whose workers, including senior scientists, are now managed by Exult. His answer: "Exult knows it has to satisfy me if it wants to keep the contract. Sure, they make the decision to fire someone or move them. But normally only because I suggested it or after they consulted with me."

Clearly, something is happening in employee relations that does not fit with what the management books still write about and what we teach in business school. And it surely does not fit with the way HR departments at most organizations were designed to function.

Strangled in Red Tape

The reason usually offered for the popularity of temporary workers is that they give employers flexibility. But far too many temps work for the same employer for long periods of time—sometimes year after year—for that to be the whole explanation. And flexibility surely does not account for the emergence of PEOs. A more plausible explanation for the popularity of these trends is that both types of organizations legally make "nonemployees" out of people who work for a business. The driving force behind the steady growth of temps and the emergence of the PEOs, I would argue, is the growing burden of rules and regulations for employers.

The cost alone of these rules and regulations threatens to strangle small businesses. According to the U.S. Small Business Administration, the annual cost of government regulations, government-required paperwork, and tax compliance for U.S. businesses employing fewer than 500 employees was somewhere around $5,000 per employee in 1995 (the last year for which reliable figures are available). That amounts to about a 25% surcharge on top of the cost of employee wages, health care, insurance, and pensions—which in 1995 was around $22,500 for the average small-business employee. Since then, the cost of employment-related paperwork is estimated to have risen by more than 10%.

Many of these costs can be avoided altogether by using temporary workers in place of traditional employees. That's why so many companies are contracting with temp agencies for workers—even though the hourly cost of a temp is often substantially higher than the wage-and-benefit cost of a full-time, formal employee. Another way to reduce the bureaucratic costs is to outsource employee relations—in other words, to let a specialist do the paperwork. Aggregating enough small businesses to manage at least 500 employees as one workforce—which is, of course, what a PEO does—can cut employment-related costs by 40%, according to SBA figures.

It is not only small businesses that can cut their labor costs substantially by outsourcing employee relations. A 1997 McKinsey study concluded that a global *Fortune* 500 firm—in other words, a very big company indeed—could cut its labor costs 25% to 33% by having its employee relations managed by an outside company. This study led to the foundation of Exult a year later.

The outsourcing of employees and employee relations is an international trend. Although employment laws and regulations vary widely from country to country, the costs they impose on businesses are high everywhere in the developed world. For instance, Adecco's biggest market is France, its second-largest market is the United States, and the company is growing at a rate of 40% per year in Japan. Exult opened an employee management center in Scotland in 2000 and has offices in London and Geneva.

Even more onerous than the costs of complying with employment laws are the enormous demands that the regulations place on management's time and attention. Between 1980 and 2000, the number of U.S. laws and regulations regarding employment policies and practices grew by about 60%, from 38 to 60. The regulations all require managers to file multiple reports, and they all threaten fines and punishment for noncompliance, even if the breach was unintentional. According to the SBA, the owner of a small or midsize business spends up to a quarter of his or her time on employment-related paperwork.

Then there is the constant, and constantly growing, threat of lawsuits: Between 1991 and 2000, the number of sexual harassment cases filed with the Equal Employment Opportunity Commission more than doubled, from about 6,900 a year to almost 16,000 a year. And for every case filed, ten or more were being settled in-house, each requiring many hours of investigation and hearings, as well as substantial legal fees.

No wonder that employers (especially smaller companies, which constitute the overwhelming majority) complain bitterly that they have no time to work on products and services, on customers and markets, on quality and distribution—that is, they have no time to work on results. Instead, they work on problems—that is, on employee regulations. They no longer chant the old mantra "People are our greatest asset." Instead, they claim "People are our greatest liability." What underlies the success of the employment agencies and the emergence of the PEOs is that they both enable management to focus on the business.

This argument, by the way, may also explain the success of *maquiladoras*—the manufacturing plants on the Mexican side of the U.S. border, and, increasingly, in Mexico proper, that assemble parts made in the United States, the Far East, or Mexico into finished products for the U.S. market. In fact, avoiding hours of paperwork is probably a stronger incentive for manufacturing companies to outsource this kind of assembly work than the often questionable savings in labor costs. The Mexican company that is the maquiladora's landlord acts as the coemployer, handling all employee regulations and activities—which are as complicated in Mexico as they are in the United States—thus freeing up the U.S. or Japanese plant owner to focus on the business.

There is not the slightest reason to believe that the costs or demands of employment rules and regulations will decrease in any developed country. Quite the contrary: No matter how badly the United States needs a patient's bill of rights, that will undoubtedly create another layer of agencies with which an employer will have to deal—another set of reports and paperwork, another avalanche of complaints, disputes, and lawsuits.

The Splintered Organization

Beyond the desire to avoid the costs and distractions of regulations, there is another major reason for both the rise of temporary workers and the emergence of PEOs: the nature of knowledge work and, most particularly, the fact that knowledge workers are extraordinarily specialized. Most large, knowledge-based organizations have lots of experts; managing all of them effectively is a big challenge— one that temp agencies and PEOs can help to address.

Not so long ago, even in the 1950s, as much as 90% of the U.S. workforce was classified as "nonexempt"—subordinates who did as they were told. The "exempt" were the supervisors who did the telling. Most nonexempt employees were blue-collar workers who had few skills and little education. They typically did repetitive tasks on the plant floor or in the office. Today, less than one-fifth of the workforce is blue-collar. Knowledge workers now make up two-fifths of the workforce, and while they may have a supervisor, they are not subordinates. They are associates. Within their area of expertise, they are supposed to do the telling.

Above all, knowledge workers are not homogeneous: Knowledge is effective only if it is specialized. This is particularly true among the fastest-growing group of knowledge workers—indeed, the fastest-growing group in the workforce overall—knowledge technologists such as computer repair people, paralegals, and software programmers. Because knowledge work is specialized, it is deeply splintered work, even in large organizations.

The best example is the hospital—altogether the most complex human organization ever devised, but also, in the past 30 or 40 years, one of the fastest-growing types of organizations in all developed countries. A fair-sized community hospital of 275 or 300 beds will have around 3,000 people working for it. Close to half of them will be knowledge workers of one kind or another. Two of these groups— nurses and specialists in the business departments—are fairly large, numbering several hundred people each. But there are about 30 paramedic specialties: physical therapists, lab workers, psychiatric caseworkers, oncological technicians, the teams of people who prepare patients for surgery, the people in the sleep clinic, the ultrasound technicians, the cardiac-clinic specialists, and many, many more.

Each of these specialties has its own rules and regulations, educational requirements, and accreditation processes. Yet in any given hospital, each specialty area comprises only a handful of people; there may be no more than seven or eight dieticians, for instance, in a 275-bed hospital. Each group, however, expects and requires special treatment. Each expects—and needs—someone higher up who understands what the group is doing, what equipment it needs, and what its relationship should be to doctors, nurses, and the business office. Also, there are no career-advancement opportunities within the hospital for any of the specialists; not one of them wants to be the hospital's administrator or has any chance of getting the job.

Few businesses currently have as many specialists as hospitals do, but they're getting there. A department store chain I know of now counts 15 or 16 distinct knowledge specialties—for instance, the retail buyers, the display people, the salespeople, and the promotions and advertising group—and employs only a handful of each kind of specialist in any one store. In financial services, too, there is increasing specialization among knowledge workers and fewer career opportunities for them within the organization. For instance, the experts who select the mutual funds to be offered to retail customers probably will not become salespeople, servicing individual accounts. And it is likely that they will not be particularly interested in managing anything larger than a small group at the firm—a handful of fellow specialists, at most.

Hospitals in the United States have largely tackled this problem of specialization through piecemeal outsourcing. In many hospitals, each knowledge specialty is managed by a different outsourcer. For instance, the group that administers blood transfusions may be managed by a company that specializes in this procedure and that simultaneously runs the transfusion departments at several other hospitals. Like a PEO, it is the coemployer of the blood transfusion staff. Within this network, the individual transfusion specialists have career opportunities: If they perform well, they can move up to manage the transfusion department at a bigger and better-paying hospital, or they can supervise several transfusion units within the network.

Both the large temp company and the PEO do across the board what in the hospital is done piecemeal. Each of their clients—even the biggest—lacks the ability to effectively manage, place, and satisfy highly specialized knowledge workers. Thus, temp firms and PEOs perform a vital function for employees as well as their employers. This explains why PEOs can claim, and apparently document, that the people whose coemployer they have become report high job satisfaction—in contradiction to everything human relations theory would have predicted. The metallurgist in a midsize chemical company may be well paid and have an interesting job, but the company needs and employs only a handful of metallurgists. No one in upper management understands what the metallurgist is doing, should be doing, could be doing. There is no opportunity, except a remote one, for the metallurgist to become an executive; that would mean giving up what he has spent years learning to do and loves to do. The well-run temp agency places the metallurgist where he can make maximum contributions. It can place the successful metallurgist in increasingly better-paid jobs.

In a PEO full-service contract (and many PEOs won't offer any other) it is expressly provided that the PEO has the duty and the right to place people in the jobs and companies where they best fit. Balancing its dual responsibilities—to the corporate client and to the employee—is probably the PEO's most important and challenging job.

Companies Don't Get It

HR policies still assume that most if not all of the people who work for a company are employees of that company. But as we have seen, that is not true. Some are temps and others are employees of the outsourcers who manage, say, the company's computer systems or call center. Still others are older part-time workers who have taken early retirement but still work on specific assignments. With all this splintering, no one is left to view the organization in its entirety.

Temp agencies claim to be selling productivity—in other words, to be doing the organization's oversight job for them—but it's hard to see how they can deliver. The productivity of the people they supply to a customer depends not only on how and where those workers are placed but also on who manages and motivates them. The temp agency has no control over those last two areas. The PEO, too, manages only its clients' formal employees, not necessarily part-time, temp, or contract workers.

This lack of oversight is a real problem. Every organization must take management responsibility for *all* the people whose productivity and performance it relies on—whether they're temps, part-timers, employees of the organization itself, or employees of its outsourcers, suppliers, and distributors.

There are signs that we are moving in that direction. A European multinational consumer goods maker is about to spin off its large and highly regarded employee management function into a separate corporation that would act as the PEO for the parent company and its employees throughout the world. This PEO would also manage the multinational's relationships with, and utilization of, people who are not traditional employees of the organization. Eventually, this in-house PEO will offer itself as the coemployer for those who work for the multinational's suppliers and distributors and for its more than 200 joint ventures and alliances.

A Source of Competitive Advantage

It is actually more important today for organizations to pay close attention to the health and well-being of all their workers than it was 50 years ago. A knowledge-based workforce is qualitatively different from a less-skilled one. True, knowledge workers are a minority of the total workforce and are unlikely ever to be more than that. But they have become the major creators of wealth and jobs. Increasingly, the success—indeed, the survival—of every business will depend on the performance of its knowledge workforce. And since it is impossible, according to the laws of statistics, for an organization to hire more than a handful of "better people," the only way that it can excel in a knowledge-based economy and society is by getting more out of the same kind of people—that is, by managing its knowledge workers for greater productivity. The challenge, to repeat an old saying, is "to make ordinary people do extraordinary things."

What made the traditional workforce productive was the system, whether it was Frederick Winslow Taylor's "one best way," Henry Ford's assembly line, or W. Edwards Deming's "total quality management." The system embodies the knowledge. The system is productive because it enables individual workers to perform without much knowledge or skill. In fact, on assembly lines and in TQM shops, a highly skilled individual can be a threat to coworkers and to the entire system. In a knowledge-based organization, however, it is the individual worker's productivity that makes the entire system successful. In a traditional workforce, the worker serves the system; in a knowledge workforce, the system must serve the worker.

There are enough knowledge-based organizations around to show what that means. What makes a university a great university is that it attracts and develops outstanding teachers and scholars, making it possible for them to do outstanding teaching and research. The same is true of an opera house. But the knowledge-based institution that most nearly resembles a knowledge-based business is the symphony orchestra, in which some 30 different instrumentalists play the same score together as a team. A great orchestra is not composed of great musicians but of adequate ones who produce at their peak. When a new conductor is hired to turn around an orchestra that has suffered years of drift and neglect, he cannot, as a rule, fire any but a few of the sloppiest or most superannuated players. He also cannot hire many new orchestra members. He has to make productive what he has inherited. The successful conductors do this by working closely with individual orchestra members and with groups of instrumentalists. The conductor's employee relations are a given; the players are nearly unchangeable. So it is the conductor's people skills that make the difference.

It would be difficult to overstate the importance of focusing on knowledge workers' productivity. The critical feature of a knowledge workforce is that its workers are not labor, they are capital. And what is decisive in the performance of capital is not what capital costs. It is not how much capital is being invested—or else the Soviet Union would have easily been the world's foremost economy. What's critical is the productivity of capital. The Soviet Union's economy collapsed, in large part, because the productivity of its capital investments was incredibly low. In many cases, it was less than one-third that of capital investments in market economies, and sometimes actually negative—consider the huge investments in farming made during the Brezhnev years. The reason for failure was simple: No one paid any attention to the productivity of capital. No one had that as his or her job. No one got rewarded if productivity went up.

Private industry in the market economies teaches the same lesson. In new industries, leadership can be obtained and maintained by innovation. In an established industry, however, what differentiates the leading company is almost always outstanding productivity of capital.

In the early part of the twentieth century, General Electric, for instance, competed with rivals like Westinghouse and Siemens through innovative technology and products. But in the early 1920s, after the era of rapid technology innovation in electromechanics had come to an end, GE concentrated on the productivity of capital to give it decisive leadership, and it has maintained this lead ever since. Similarly, Sears's glory days from the late 1920s through the 1960s were not based on its merchandise or pricing—the company's rivals, such as Montgomery Ward, did just as well in both areas. Sears prevailed because it got about twice as much work out of a dollar as other American retailers did. Knowledge-based businesses need to be similarly focused on the productivity of their capital—that is, the productivity of the knowledge worker.

Free Managers to Manage People

Temps and especially PEOs free up managers to focus on the business rather than on employment-related rules, regulations, and paperwork. To spend up to one-quarter of one's time on employment-related paperwork is indeed a waste of precious, expensive, scarce resources. It is boring. It demeans and corrupts, and the only thing it can possibly teach is greater skill in cheating.

Companies thus have ample reason to try to do away with the routine chores of employee relations—whether by systematizing employee management in-house or by outsourcing it to temps or to a PEO. But they need to be careful that they don't damage or destroy their relationships with people in the process. Indeed, the main benefit of decreasing paperwork may be to gain more time for people relations. Executives will have to learn what the effective department head in the university or the successful conductor of the symphony orchestra have long known: The key to greatness is to look for people's potential and spend time developing it. To build an outstanding university department requires spending time with the promising young postdocs and assistant professors until they excel in their work. To build a world-class orchestra requires rehearsing the same passage in the symphony again and again until the first clarinet plays it the way the conductor hears it. This principle is also what makes a research director in an industry lab successful.

Similarly, leaders in knowledge-based businesses must spend time with promising professionals: Get to know them and be known by them; mentor them and listen to them; challenge them and encourage them. Even if these people are not traditional—read, legal—employees, they are still a capital resource for the organization and critical to its business performance. The administrative tasks that are involved with employee relations can, and should, be systematized—and that means they can, perhaps should, become impersonal. But if employee relations are being outsourced, executives need to work closely with their PEO counterparts on the professional development, motivation, satisfaction, and productivity of the knowledge workers on whose performance their own results depend.

Modern organizations emerged from the Industrial Revolution. The cotton mill and the railroad were first. But while unprecedented, they were still based on manual labor, as was all earlier work, whether it was farming, manufacturing, clearing checks by hand, or entering life-insurance claims into a ledger. This was the case as late as 50 or 60 years ago, even in the most highly developed economies. The emergence of knowledge work and the knowledge worker—let alone their emergence as the chief source of capital in our knowledge-based society and economy—is thus as profound a change as the switch to a machine-driven economy was all those years ago, perhaps an even greater one.

This shift will require more than just a few new programs and a few new practices. It will require new measurements, new values, new goals, and new policies. It will predictably take a good many years before we have worked these out. However, there are enough successful knowledge-based organizations around to tell us what the basic assumption has to be for managing employees in today's companies: Employees may be our greatest liability, but people are our greatest opportunity.

Originally published in February 2002. Reprint R0202E

The New Productivity Challenge

THE SINGLE GREATEST CHALLENGE facing managers in the developed countries of the world is to raise the productivity of knowledge and service workers. This challenge, which will dominate the management agenda for the next several decades, will ultimately determine the competitive performance of companies. Even more important, it will determine the very fabric of society and the quality of life in every industrialized nation.

For the last 120 years, productivity in making and moving things—in manufacturing, farming, mining, construction, and transportation—has risen in developed countries at an annual rate of 3% to 4%, a 45-fold expansion overall. On this explosive growth rest all the gains these nations and their citizens have enjoyed: vast increases in disposable income and purchasing power; ever-wider access to education and health care; and the availability of leisure time, something known only to aristocrats and the "idle rich" before 1914, when everyone else worked at least 3,000 hours a year. (Today even the Japanese work no more than about 2,000 hours each year, while Americans average 1,800 hours and West Germans 1,650.)

Now these gains are unraveling, but not because productivity in making and moving things has fallen. Contrary to popular belief, productivity in these activities is still going up at much the same rate. And it is rising fully as much in the United States as it is in Japan or West Germany. Indeed, the increase in U.S. manufacturing productivity during the 1980s—some 3.9% a year—was actually larger in absolute terms than the corresponding annual increases in Japan and Germany, while the 4% to 5% annual rise in U.S. agricultural productivity is far and away the largest recorded anywhere at any time.

The productivity revolution is over because there are too few people employed in making and moving things for their productivity to be decisive. All told, they account for no more than one-fifth of the work force in developed economies. Only 30 years ago, they were still a near-majority. Even Japan, which is still manufacturing intensive, can no longer expect increased productivity in that sector to sustain its economic growth. Indeed, the great majority of working people in Japan are knowledge and service workers with productivities as low as those in any other developed country. And when farmers make up only 3% of the employed population, as they do in the United States, Japan, and most of Western Europe, even record increases in their output add virtually nothing to their country's overall productivity and wealth.

The chief *economic* priority for developed countries, therefore, must be to raise the productivity of knowledge and service work. The country that does this first will dominate the twenty-first century economically. The most pressing *social* challenge developed countries face, however, will be to raise the productivity of service work. Unless this challenge is met, the developed world will face increasing social tensions, increasing polarization, increasing radicalization, possibly even class war.

In developed economies, opportunities for careers and promotion are more and more limited to people with advanced schooling, people qualified for knowledge work. But these men and women will always be a minority. They will always be outnumbered by people who lack the qualifications for anything but low-skilled service jobs—people who in their social position are comparable to the "proletarians" of 100 years ago, the poorly educated, unskilled

Idea in Brief

One hundred years ago, Frederick Taylor set off a revolution that ultimately defeated Marx. By studying how the work of making and moving things could be performed most effectively, Taylor laid the foundation for gains in manufacturing productivity that allowed common laborers to earn the wages of skilled craftsmen.

Today, developed economies need another productivity revolution—this time in knowledge and service work. The country that first achieves such productivity gains will dominate the next century economically. Countries that fail—particularly with respect to service workers—will face rising social tensions, if not class war.

The key to this new productivity revolution is what Taylor called "working smarter." Applied to knowledge and service work, working smarter requires five distinct steps:

- Define the task. Ask about each job not only "What are we trying to accomplish?" but also "Must we do it at all?" The easiest productivity gains come from eliminating what does not need to be done.

- Concentrate on the task. Too much "job enrichment" takes the form of busywork, diverting employees from work that adds value.

- Define performance. For some jobs, performance means quality. For a second set of jobs, quality and quantity constitute performance. Finally, some service jobs are "production" jobs, in which performance is largely defined by the quantity of work accomplished, and quality is a matter of external criteria.

- Ask the people who do the work how they think their productivity can be improved. Today's managers have to work in partnership with employees.

- Build continuous learning into the organization through training and by asking performers to become teachers for the rest.

masses who thronged the exploding industrial cities and streamed into their factories.

In the early 1880s, intelligent observers of every political persuasion were obsessed with the specter of class war between the industrial proletariat and the bourgeoisie. Karl Marx was hardly alone in predicting that the "immiserization" of the proletariat would lead inevitably to revolution. Benjamin Disraeli, perhaps the greatest of the nineteenth century conservatives, was equally persuaded of the inevitability of class war. And Henry James, the chronicler of American wealth and European aristocracy, was so frightened by the prospect that he made it the central theme of *The Princess Casamassima,* one of his most haunting novels.

What defeated these prophecies, which seemed eminently reasonable, indeed almost self-evident to contemporaries, was the revolution in productivity set off by Frederick W. Taylor in 1881, when he began to study the way a common laborer shoveled sand. Taylor himself worked in an iron foundry and was deeply shocked by the bitter animosity between the workers and managers. Fearful that this hatred would ultimately lead to class war, he set out to improve the efficiency of industrial work. And his efforts, in turn, sparked the revolution that allowed industrial workers to earn middle-class wages and achieve middle-class status despite their lack of skill and education. By 1930, when according to Marx the revolution of the proletariat should have been a fait accompli, the proletariat had become the bourgeoisie.

Now it is time for another productivity revolution. This time, however, history is on our side. In the past century, we have learned a great deal about productivity and how to raise it—enough to know that we need a revolution, enough to know how to start one.

––––––––––––

Knowledge and service workers range from research scientists and cardiac surgeons through draftswomen and store managers to 16-year-olds who flip hamburgers in fast-food restaurants on Saturday afternoons. Their ranks also include people whose work makes them "machine operators": dishwashers, janitors, data-entry operators. Yet for all their diversity in knowledge, skill, responsibility, social status, and pay, knowledge and service workers are remarkably alike in two crucial respects: what does not work in raising their productivity and what does.

The first thing we have learned—and it came as a rude shock—is about what does not work. Capital cannot be substituted for labor. Nor will new technology by itself generate higher productivity. In making and moving things, capital and technology are *factors* of production, to use the economist's term. In knowledge and service work, they are *tools* of production. The difference is that a factor can replace labor, while a tool may or may not. Whether tools help productivity or harm it depends on what people do with them, on the purpose to which they are being put, for instance, or on the skill of the user. Thirty years ago, for example, we were sure the efficiency of the computer would lead to massive reductions in clerical and office staff. The promise of greater productivity led to massive investments in data-processing equipment that now rival those in materials-processing technology (that is, in conventional machinery). Yet office and clerical forces have grown at a much faster rate since the introduction of information technology than ever before. And there has been virtually no increase in the productivity of service work.

Hospitals are a telling example. In the late 1940s, they were entirely labor intensive, with little capital investment except in bricks, mortar, and beds. A good many perfectly respectable hospitals had not even invested in readily available, fairly old technologies: they provided neither x-ray departments nor clinical laboratories nor physical therapy. Today hospitals are hugely capital intensive, with enormous sums invested in ultrasound, body scanners, nuclear magnetic imagers, blood and tissue analyzers, clean rooms, and a dozen more new technologies. Each piece of equipment has brought with it the need for more highly paid people but has not reduced the existing staff by a single person. (In fact, the worldwide escalation of health-care costs is largely the result of the hospital's having become a labor-intensive and capital-intensive monstrosity.) But hospitals, at least, have significantly increased their performance capacity. In other areas of knowledge or service work there are only higher costs, more investment, and more people.

Massive increases in productivity are the only way out of this morass. And these increases can only come from what Taylor called "working smarter."[1] Simply, this means working more productively without working harder or longer.

The economist sees capital investment as the key to productivity; the technologist gives star billing to new machines. Nevertheless, the main force behind the productivity explosion has been working smarter. Capital investment and technology were as copious in the developed economies during the first 100 years of the Industrial Revolution as they have been in its second 100 years. It was only with the advent of working smarter that productivity in making and moving things took off on its meteoric rise.

And so it will be for knowledge and service work—with this difference: in manufacturing, working smarter is only one key to increased productivity. In knowledge and service work, working smarter is the only key. What is more, it is a more complex key, one that requires looking closely at work in ways that Taylor never dreamed of.

When Taylor studied the shoveling of sand, the only question that concerned him was, "How is it done?" Almost 50 years later, when Harvard's Elton Mayo set out to demolish Taylor's "scientific management" and replace it with what later came to be called "human relations," he focused on the same question. In his experiments at Western Electric's Hawthorne Works, Mayo asked, "How can wiring telephone equipment best be done?" The point is that in making and moving things, the task is always taken for granted.

In knowledge and service work, however, the first questions in increasing productivity—and working smarter—have to be, "What is the task? What are we trying to accomplish? Why do it at all?" The easiest, but perhaps also the greatest, productivity gains in such work will come from defining the task and especially from eliminating what does not need to be done.[2]

A very old example is still one of the best: mail-order processing at the early Sears, Roebuck. Between 1906 and 1908, Sears eliminated the time-consuming job of counting the money in incoming mail orders. Rather than open the money envelopes enclosed with the orders, Sears weighed them automatically. In those days, virtually all Sears customers paid with coins. If the weight of the envelope tallied with the amount of the order within fairly narrow limits, the envelope went unopened. Similarly, Sears eliminated the even more time-consuming task of recording each incoming order by scheduling order handling and shipping according to the weight of the incoming mail (assuming 40 orders for each pound of mail).

Within two years, these steps accounted for a tenfold increase in the productivity of the entire mail-order operation.[3]

A major insurance company recently increased the productivity of its claims-settlement department nearly fivefold—from an average of 15 minutes per claim to 3 minutes—by eliminating detailed checking on all but very large claims. Instead of verifying 30 items as they had always done, the adjusters now check only 4: whether the policy is still in force; whether the face amount matches the amount of the claim; whether the name of the policyholder matches the name on the death certificate; and whether the name of the beneficiary matches the name of the claimant. What provoked the change was asking, "What is the task?" and then answering, "To pay death claims as fast and as cheaply as possible." All that the company now requires to control the process is to work through a 2% sample, that is, every fiftieth claim, the traditional way.

Similarly, a few hospitals have taken most of the labor and expense out of their admissions process by admitting all patients the way they used to admit emergency cases who were brought in unconscious or bleeding and unable to fill out lengthy forms. These hospitals asked, "What is the task?" and answered, "To identify the patient's name, sex, age, address and how to bill"—information found on the insurance identification cards practically all patients carry.

These are both examples of service work. In knowledge work, defining the task and getting rid of what does not need to be done is even more necessary and produces even greater results. Consider how one multinational company redefined its strategic planning.

For many years, a planning staff of 45 brilliant people carefully prepared strategic scenarios in minute detail. The documents were first-class works and made stimulating reading, everybody agreed. But they had a minimal impact on operations. Then a new CEO asked, "What is the task?" and answered, "To give our businesses direction and goals and the strategy to attain these goals." It took four years of hard work and several false starts. But now the planning people (still about the same number) work through only three questions for each of the company's businesses: What market standing does it need to maintain leadership? What innovative performance does it need to support that standing? And what is the minimum rate of return needed to earn the cost of capital? Then the planning people work with the operating executives in each business to map out broad strategic guidelines for achieving these goals under various economic conditions. The results are far simpler and much less elegant, but they have become the "flight plans" that guide the company's businesses and its senior executives.

When people make or move things, they do one task at a time. Taylor's laborer shoveled sand; he did not also stoke the furnace. Mayo's wiring-room women soldered; they did not test finished telephones on the side. The Iowa farmer planting corn does not get off his tractor between rows to attend a meeting. Knowledge and service work, too, require concentration. The surgeon does not take telephone calls in the operating room, nor does the lawyer in consultation with a client.

But in organizations, where most knowledge and service work takes place, splintered attention is more and more the norm. The people at the very top can sometimes concentrate themselves (though far too few even try). But the great majority of engineers, teachers, salespeople, nurses, middle managers, and the like must carry a steadily growing load of busywork, activities that contribute little if any value and that have little if anything to do with what these professionals are qualified and paid for.

The worst case may be that of nurses in U.S. hospitals. We hear a great deal about the shortage of nurses. But how could it possibly be true? The number of graduates entering the profession has gone up steadily for a good many years. At the same time, the number of bed patients has been dropping sharply. The explanation of the paradox: nurses now spend only half their time doing what they have learned and are paid to do—nursing. The other half is eaten up by activities that do not require their skill and knowledge, add neither health-care nor economic value, and have little or nothing to do with patient care and patient well-being. Nurses are preoccupied, of course, with the avalanche of paperwork for Medicare, Medicaid, insurers, the billing office, and the prevention of malpractice suits.

The situation in higher education is not too different. Faculty in colleges and universities spend more and more hours in committee meetings instead of teaching in the classroom, advising students, or doing research. But few of these committees would ever be missed. And they would do a better job in less time if they had three instead of seven members.

Salespeople are just as splintered. In department stores, they now spend so much time serving computers that they have little time for serving customers—the main reason, perhaps, for the steady decline in their productivity as producers of sales and revenues. Field-sales representatives spend up to one-third of their time filling out reports rather than calling on customers. And engineers sit through meeting after meeting when they should be busy at their workstations.

This is not job enrichment; it is job impoverishment. It destroys productivity. It saps motivation and morale. Nurses, every attitude survey shows, bitterly resent not being able to spend more time caring for patients. They also believe, understandably, that they are grossly underpaid for what they are capable of doing, while the hospital administrator, equally understandably, believes that they are grossly overpaid for the unskilled clerical work they are actually doing.

The cure is fairly easy, as a rule. It is to concentrate the work— in this case, nursing—on the task—caring for patients. This is the second step toward working smarter. A few hospitals, for example, have taken the paperwork out of the nurse's job and given it to a floor clerk who also answers telephone calls from relatives and friends and arranges the flowers they send in. The level of patient care and the hours nurses devote to it have risen sharply. Yet the hospitals have also been able to reduce their nursing staffs by one-quarter or one-third and so raise salaries without incurring a higher nursing payroll.

To make these kinds of improvements, we must ask a second set of questions about every knowledge and service job: "What do we pay for? What value is this job supposed to add?" The answer is not always obvious or noncontroversial. One department store looked at its sales force and answered "sales," while another in the same metropolitan area and with much the same clientele answered "customer service." Each answer led to a different restructuring of the jobs on the sales floor. But each store achieved, and fairly fast, substantial growth in the revenues each salesperson and each department generated, that is, gains in both productivity and profitability.

For all its tremendous impact, Taylor's scientific management has had a bad press, especially in academia. Perhaps the main reason is the unrelenting campaign U.S. labor unions waged against it—and against Taylor himself—in the early years of this century. The unions did not oppose Taylor because they thought him antilabor or promanagement. He was neither. His unforgivable sin was his assertion that there is no such thing as "skill" in making and moving things. All such work was the same, Taylor asserted. And all could be analyzed step by step, as a series of unskilled operations that could then be combined into any kind of job. Anyone willing to learn these operations would be a "first-class man," deserving "first-class pay." He could do the most advanced work and do it to perfection.

To the skill-based unions of 1900, this assertion represented a direct attack. And this was especially true for the highly respected, extremely powerful unions that dominated what were then some of the country's most sophisticated manufacturing sites—the army arsenals and navy shipyards where nearly all peacetime production for the military took place until well after World World I. For these unions, each craft was a mystery whose secrets no member could divulge. Their power base was control of an apprenticeship that lasted five or seven years and admitted, as a rule, only relatives of members. And their workers were paid extremely well—more than most physicians of the day and triple what Taylor's first-class man could expect to get. No wonder that Taylor's assertions infuriated these aristocrats of labor.

Belief in the mystery of craft and skill persisted, as did the assumption that long years of apprenticeship were needed to acquire both. Indeed, Hitler went to war with the United States on the strength of that assumption. Convinced that it took five years or more to train optical craftsmen (whose skills are essential to modern warfare), he thought it would be at least that long before America could field an effective army and air force in Europe—and so declared war after the Japanese attack on Pearl Harbor.

We know now Taylor was right. The United States had almost no optical craftsmen in 1941. And modern warfare indeed requires precision optics in large quantities. But by applying Taylor's methods of scientific management, within a few months the United States trained semiskilled workers to turn out more highly advanced optics than even the Germans were producing, and on an assembly line to boot. And by that time, Taylor's first-class men with their increased productivity were also making a great deal more money than any craftsman of 1911 had ever dreamed of.

Eventually, knowledge work and service work may turn out to be like the work of making and moving things—that is, "just work," to use an old scientific management slogan. (At least this is what Taylor's true heirs, the more radical proponents of artificial intelligence, maintain.) But for the time being, we must not treat knowledge and service jobs as "just work." Nor can we assume they are homogeneous. Rather, these jobs can be divided into three distinct categories by looking at what productive performance in a given job actually represents. This process—defining performance—is the third step toward working smarter.

For some knowledge and service jobs, performance means quality. Take scientists in a research lab where quantity—the number of results—is quite secondary to their quality. One new drug that can generate annual sales of $500 million and dominate the market for a decade is infinitely more valuable than 20 "me too" drugs with annual sales of $20 million or $30 million each. The same principle applies to basic policy or strategic decisions, as well as to much less grandiose work, the physician's diagnosis, for example, or packaging design, or editing a magazine. In each of these instances, we do not yet know how to analyze the process that produces quality results. To raise productivity, therefore, we can only ask, "What works?"

The second category includes the majority of knowledge and service work: jobs in which quality and quantity together constitute performance. Department store sales are one example. Producing a "satisfied customer" is just as important as the dollar amount on the sales slip, but it is not so easy to define. Likewise, the quality of an architectural draftswoman's work is an integral part of her performance. But so is the number of drawings she can produce. The same holds true for engineers, sales reps in brokerage offices, medical technologists, branch bank managers, reporters, nurses, claims adjusters, and so on. Raising productivity in these jobs requires asking, "What works?" but also analyzing the process step by step and operation by operation.

Finally, there are a good many service jobs (filing, handling death claims, making hospital beds) in which performance is defined much as it is in making and moving things: that is, largely by quantity (for example, the number of minutes it takes to make up a hospital bed properly). In these "production" jobs, quality is primarily a matter of external criteria rather than an attribute of performance itself. Defining standards and building them into the work process is essential. But once this has been done, real productivity improvements will come through conventional industrial engineering, that is, through analyzing the task and combining the individual simple operations into a complete job.

Defining the task, concentrating work on the task, and defining performance: by themselves, these three steps will produce substantial growth in productivity—perhaps most of what can be attained at any one time. They will need to be worked through again and again, maybe as often as every three or five years and certainly whenever work or its organization changes. But then, according to all the experience we have, the resulting productivity increases will equal, if not exceed, whatever industrial engineering, scientific management, or human relations ever achieved in manufacturing. In other words, they should give us the productivity revolution we need in knowledge and service work.

But on one condition only: that we apply what we have learned since World War II about increasing productivity in making and moving things. The fourth step toward working smarter, then, is for management to form a partnership with the people who hold the jobs, the people who are to become more productive. The goal has to be to build responsibility for productivity and performance into every knowledge and service job regardless of level, difficulty, or skill.

Frederick Taylor has often been criticized for never once asking the workers he studied how they thought their jobs could be improved. He told them. Nor did Elton Mayo ever ask; he also told. But Taylor's (and Mayo's, 40 years later) methodology was simply a product of the times, when the wisdom of the expert prevailed. (Freud, after all, never asked his patients what they thought their problems might be. Nor do we have any record that either Marx or Lenin ever thought of asking the masses.) Taylor considered both workers and managers "dumb oxen." And while Mayo had great respect for managers, he thought workers were "immature" and "maladjusted," deeply in need of the psychologist's expert guidance.

When World War II came, however, we had to ask the workers. We had no choice. U.S. factories had no engineers, psychologists, or foremen. They were all in uniform. To our immense surprise, as I still recollect, we discovered that the workers were neither dumb oxen nor immature nor maladjusted. They knew a great deal about the work they were doing—about its logic and rhythm, its quality, and its tools. Asking them what they thought was the way to address both productivity and quality.[4]

At first, only a few businesses accepted this novel proposition. (IBM was a pioneer and for a long time one of the few large companies to act on this idea.) But in the late 1950s and early 1960s, it was picked up by Japanese industrialists whose earlier attempts to return to prewar autocracy had collapsed in bloody strikes and near-civil war. Now, while still far from being widely practiced, it is at least generally accepted in theory that the workers' knowledge of their job is the starting point for improving productivity, quality, and performance.

In making and moving things, however, partnership with the responsible worker is only the *best* way to increase productivity. After all, Taylor's telling worked too, and quite well. In knowledge and service work, partnership with the responsible worker is the *only* way.

The last component of working smarter is a two-part lesson that neither Taylor nor Mayo knew. First, continuous learning must accompany productivity gains. Redesigning a job and then teaching the worker the new way to do it, which is what Taylor did and taught, cannot by itself sustain ongoing learning. Training is only the beginning of learning. Indeed, as the Japanese can teach us (thanks to their ancient tradition of Zen), the greatest benefit of training comes not from learning something new but from doing better what we already do well.

Equally important is a related insight of the last few years: knowledge workers and service workers learn most when they teach. The best way to improve a star salesperson's productivity is to ask her to present "the secret of my success" at the company sales convention. The best way for the surgeon to improve his performance is to give a talk about it at the county medical society. We often hear it said that in the information age, every enterprise has to become a learning institution. It must become a teaching institution as well.

One hundred years ago, the signs of class conflict were unmistakable. What defused that conflict—and averted class war—was growth in the productivity of the industrial work force, something so unprecedented that even its prime mover, Frederick Taylor, had no term to describe it.

Today we know that productivity is the true source of competitive advantage. But what we must also realize is that it is the key to social stability as well. For that reason, achieving gains in service productivity comparable with those we have already achieved in manufacturing productivity must be a priority for managers throughout the developed world.

It is an economic truth that real incomes cannot be higher than productivity for any extended length of time. Unless the productivity of service workers rapidly improves, both the social and the economic position of that large group of people—whose numbers rival those of manufacturing workers at their peak—must steadily go down. At a minimum, this raises the prospect of economic stagnation; more ominously, it raises the prospect of social tensions unmatched since the early decades of the Industrial Revolution.

Conceivably, service workers could use their numerical strength to get higher wages than their economic contribution justifies. But this would only impoverish all of society, dragging everyone's real income down and sending unemployment up. Alternatively, the income of unskilled and semiskilled service workers could continue to fall in relation to the steadily rising wages of affluent knowledge workers. But this would lead to an even wider gulf between the two groups as well as to increasing polarization. In either case, service workers can only become increasingly bitter, alienated, and ready to see themselves as a class apart.

Fortunately, we are in a much better position than our ancestors were a century ago. We know what Marx and his contemporaries did not know: productivity can be raised. We also know how to raise it. And we know this best for the work where the social need is most urgent: unskilled and semiskilled service work—maintenance jobs in factories, schools, hospitals, and offices; counter jobs in restaurants and supermarkets; clerical jobs in insurance companies, banks, and businesses of all kinds. In essence, this is production work. And what we have learned during the past 100 years about increasing productivity applies to such work with a minimum of adaptation.

Further, a model of sorts exists in the steps some multinational maintenance companies have already taken to improve their employees' productivity. These U.S. and European employers have systematically applied the approach this article discusses to low-skilled service jobs. They have defined the task, concentrated work on it, defined performance, made the employee a partner in productivity improvement and the first source of ideas for it, and built continuous learning and continuing teaching into the job of every employee and work team. As a result, they have raised productivity substantially—in some cases even doubled it—which has allowed them to raise wages. As important, this process has also greatly raised the workers' self-respect and pride.

It is no coincidence that outside contractors achieved these improvements. Obtaining major productivity gains in production-type service work usually requires contracting it out to a company that has no other business, understands this work, respects it, and offers opportunities for low-skilled workers to advance (for example, to become local or regional managers). The organizations in which this work is being done, the hospitals that own the beds, for instance, or the colleges whose students need to be fed, neither understand it nor respect it enough to devote the time and hard work that are required to make it more productive.

The task is known and doable. But the urgency is great. To raise the productivity of service work, we cannot rely on government or on politics altogether. It is the task of managers and executives in businesses and nonprofit organizations. It is, in fact, the first social responsibility of management in the knowledge society.

Originally published in November–December 1991. Reprint 91605

Notes

1. Among the few attempts to apply working smarter in health care are Roxanne Spitzer's *Nursing Productivity: The Hospital's Key to Survival and Profit* (Chicago: S-N Publications, 1986) and Regina Herzlinger's *Creating New Health Care Ventures* (Gaithersburg, Md.: Aspen Publishers, 1991).

2. See Michael Hammer, "Reengineering Work: Don't Automate, Obliterate," HBR July–August 1990, and Peter F. Drucker, "Permanent Cost Cutting," *Wall Street Journal*, January 11, 1991.

3. See Boris Emmet and John E. Jeucks, *Catalogues and Counters: A History of Sears, Roebuck & Company* (Chicago: University of Chicago Press, 1965).

4. In my 1942 book, *The Future of Industrial Man* (Westport, Conn.: Greenwood, 1978 reprint of original), and my 1950 book, *The New Society* (Greenwood, 1982 reprint), I argued for the "responsible worker" as "part of management." Edwards W. Deming and Joseph M. Juran developed what we now call "quality circles" and "total quality management" as a result of their wartime experiences. Finally, the idea was forcefully presented by Douglas McGregor in his 1960 book, *The Human Side of Enterprise* (New York: McGraw Hill, 1985, twenty-fifth anniversary printing), with its "Theory X" and "Theory Y."

What Business
Can Learn from
Nonprofits

THE GIRL SCOUTS, THE RED CROSS, the pastoral churches—our non-profit organizations—are becoming America's management leaders. In two areas, strategy and the effectiveness of the board, they are practicing what most American businesses only preach. And in the most crucial area—the motivation and productivity of knowledge workers—they are truly pioneers, working out the policies and practices that business will have to learn tomorrow.

Few people are aware that the nonprofit sector is by far America's largest employer. Every other adult—a total of 80 million plus people—works as a volunteer, giving on average nearly five hours each week to one or several nonprofit organizations. This is equal to 10 million full-time jobs. Were volunteers paid, their wages, even at minimum rate, would amount to some $150 billion, or 5% of GNP. And volunteer work is changing fast. To be sure, what many do requires little skill or judgment: collecting in the neighborhood for the Community Chest one Saturday afternoon a year, chaperoning youngsters selling Girl Scout cookies door to door, driving old people to the doctor. But more and more volunteers are becoming "unpaid staff," taking over the professional and managerial tasks in their organizations.

Not all nonprofits have been doing well, of course. A good many community hospitals are in dire straits. Traditional churches and synagogues of all persuasions—liberal, conservative, evangelical, fundamentalist—are still steadily losing members. Indeed, the sector overall has not expanded in the last 10 or 15 years, either in terms of the money it raises (when adjusted for inflation) or in the number of volunteers. Yet in its productivity, in the scope of its work and in its contribution to American society, the nonprofit sector has grown tremendously in the last two decades.

The Salvation Army is an example. People convicted to their first prison term in Florida, mostly very poor black or Hispanic youths, are now paroled into the Salvation Army's custody—about 25,000 each year. Statistics show that if these young men and women go to jail the majority will become habitual criminals. But the Salvation Army has been able to rehabilitate 80% of them through a strict work program run largely by volunteers. And the program costs a fraction of what it would to keep the offenders behind bars.

Underlying this program and many other effective nonprofit endeavors is a commitment to management. Twenty years ago, management was a dirty word for those involved in nonprofit organizations. It meant business, and nonprofits prided themselves on being free of the taint of commercialism and above such sordid considerations as the bottom line. Now most of them have learned that nonprofits need management even more than business does, precisely because they lack the discipline of the bottom line. The nonprofits are, of course, still dedicated to "doing good." But they also realize that good intentions are no substitute for organization and leadership, for accountability, performance, and results. Those require management and that, in turn, begins with the organization's mission.

As a rule, nonprofits are more money-conscious than business enterprises are. They talk and worry about money much of the time because it is so hard to raise and because they always have so much less of it than they need. But nonprofits do not base their strategy on

Idea in Brief

Every year in Florida, some 25,000 young people who have been convicted to their first term in prison enter the Salvation Army's parole program. Statistics show that if these men and women go to jail, the majority will become habitual criminals. The Salvation Army has been able to rehabilitate 80% of them through a strict work program run largely by volunteers. The program costs a fraction of what it would to keep offenders behind bars.

This kind of effectiveness is characteristic of the best nonprofit organizations. Twenty years ago, management was a dirty word in nonprofits. Today they offer best practice in two areas, strategy and effective use of the board. And in the area that presents the biggest challenge

for every enterprise—motivating knowledge workers and raising their productivity—they are truly pioneers.

In successful nonprofit enterprises, well-meaning amateurs are giving way to unpaid staff members, many of whom work as managers and professionals in their for-pay jobs. These people volunteer because they believe in the organization's mission. They stay because the organization knows how to put their competence and knowledge to work. The formula is the same, whether the employer is a church, the Girl Scouts, or a business: give people responsibility for meaningful tasks, hold them accountable for their performance, reward them with training and the chance to take on more demanding assignments.

money, nor do they make it the center of their plans, as so many corporate executives do. "The businesses I work with start their planning with financial returns," says one well-known CEO who sits on both business and nonprofit boards. "The nonprofits start with the performance of their mission."

Starting with the mission and its requirements may be the first lesson business can learn from successful nonprofits. It focuses the organization on action. It defines the specific strategies needed to attain the crucial goals. It creates a disciplined organization. It alone can prevent the most common degenerative disease of organizations, especially large ones: splintering their always limited resources on things that are "interesting" or look "profitable" rather than concentrating them on a very small number of productive efforts.

The best nonprofits devote a great deal of thought to defining their organization's mission. They avoid sweeping statements full of good intentions and focus, instead, on objectives that have clear-cut implications for the work their members perform—staff and volunteers both. The Salvation Army's goal, for example, is to turn society's rejects—alcoholics, criminals, derelicts—into citizens. The Girl Scouts help youngsters become confident, capable young women who respect themselves and other people. The Nature Conservancy preserves the diversity of nature's fauna and flora. Nonprofits also start with the environment, the community, the "customers" to be; they do not, as American businesses tend to do, start with the inside, that is, with the organization or with financial returns.

Willowcreek Community Church in South Barrington, Illinois, outside Chicago, has become the nation's largest church—some 13,000 parishioners. Yet it is barely 15 years old. Bill Hybels, in his early twenties when he founded the church, chose the community because it had relatively few churchgoers, though the population was growing fast and churches were plentiful. He went from door to door asking, "Why don't you go to church?" Then he designed a church to answer the potential customers' needs: for instance, it offers full services on Wednesday evenings because many working parents need Sunday to spend with their children. Moreover, Hybels continues to listen and react. The pastor's sermon is taped while it is being delivered and instantly reproduced so that parishioners can pick up a cassette when they leave the building because he was told again and again, "I need to listen when I drive home or drive to work so that I can build the message into my life." But he was also told: "The sermon always tells me to change my life but never how to do it." So now every one of Hybels's sermons ends with specific action recommendations.

A well-defined mission serves as a constant reminder of the need to look outside the organization not only for "customers" but also for measures of success. The temptation to content oneself with the "goodness of our cause"—and thus to substitute good intentions for results—always exists in nonprofit organizations. It is precisely because of this that the successful and performing nonprofits have learned to define clearly what changes *outside* the organization constitute "results" and to focus on them.

The experience of one large Catholic hospital chain in the Southwest shows how productive a clear sense of mission and a focus on results can be. Despite the sharp cuts in Medicare payments and hospital stays during the past eight years, this chain has increased revenues by 15% (thereby managing to break even) while greatly expanding its services and raising both patient-care and medical standards. It has done so because the nun who is its CEO understood that she and her staff are in the business of delivering health care (especially to the poor), not running hospitals.

As a result, when health care delivery began moving out of hospitals for medical rather than economic reasons about ten years ago, the chain promoted the trend instead of fighting it. It founded ambulatory surgery centers, rehabilitation centers, X-ray and lab networks, HMOs, and so on. The chain's motto was: "If it's in the patient's interest, we have to promote it; it's then our job to make it pay." Paradoxically, the policy has filled the chain's hospitals; the freestanding facilities are so popular they generate a steady stream of referrals.

This is, of course, not so different from the marketing strategy of successful Japanese companies. But it is very different indeed from the way most Western businesses think and operate. And the difference is that the Catholic nuns—and the Japanese—start with the mission rather than with their own rewards, and with what they have to make happen outside themselves, in the marketplace, to deserve a reward.

Finally, a clearly defined mission will foster innovative ideas and help others understand why they need to be implemented—however much they fly in the face of tradition. To illustrate, consider the Daisy Scouts, a program for five-year-olds which the Girl Scouts initiated a few years back. For 75 years, first grade had been the minimum age for entry into a Brownie troop, and many Girl Scout councils wanted to keep it that way. Others, however, looked at demographics and saw the growing numbers of working women with "latch key" kids. They also looked at the children and realized that they were far more sophisticated than their predecessors a generation ago (largely thanks to TV).

Today the Daisy Scouts are 100,000 strong and growing fast. It is by far the most successful of the many programs for preschoolers that have been started these last 20 years, and far more successful than any of the very expensive government programs. Moreover, it is so far the only program that has seen these critical demographic changes and children's exposure to long hours of TV viewing as an opportunity.

Many nonprofits now have what is still the exception in business—a functioning board. They also have something even rarer: a CEO who is clearly accountable to the board and whose performance is reviewed annually by a board committee. And they have what is rarer still: a board whose performance is reviewed annually against preset performance objectives. Effective use of the board is thus a second area in which business can learn from the nonprofit sector.

In U.S. law, the board of directors is still considered the "managing" organ of the corporation. Management authors and scholars agree that strong boards are essential and have been writing to that effect for more than 20 years, beginning with Myles Mace's pioneering work.[1] Nevertheless, the top managements of our large companies have been whittling away at the directors' role, power, and independence for more than half a century. In every single business failure of a large company in the last few decades, the board was the last to realize that things were going wrong. To find a truly effective board, you are much better advised to look in the nonprofit sector than in our public corporations.

In part, this difference is a product of history. Traditionally, the board has run the shop in nonprofit organizations—or tried to. In fact, it is only because nonprofits have grown too big and complex to be run by part-time outsiders, meeting for three hours a month, that so many have shifted to professional management. The American Red Cross is probably the largest nongovernmental agency in the world and certainly one of the most complex. It is responsible for worldwide disaster relief; it runs thousands of blood banks as well as the bone and skin banks in hospitals; it conducts training in cardiac and respiratory rescue nationwide; and it gives first-aid courses in thousands of schools. Yet it did not have a paid chief executive until 1950, and its first professional CEO came only with the Reagan era.

But however common professional management becomes—and professional CEOs are now found in most nonprofits and all the bigger ones—nonprofit boards cannot, as a rule, be rendered impotent the way so many business boards have been. No matter how much nonprofit CEOs would welcome it—and quite a few surely would—nonprofit boards cannot become their rubber stamp. Money is one reason. Few directors in publicly held corporations are substantial shareholders, whereas directors on nonprofit boards very often contribute large sums themselves, and are expected to bring in donors as well. But also, nonprofit directors tend to have a personal commitment to the organization's cause. Few people sit on a church vestry or on a school board unless they deeply care about religion or education. Moreover, nonprofit board members typically have served as volunteers themselves for a good many years and are deeply knowledgeable about the organization, unlike outside directors in a business.

Precisely because the nonprofit board is so committed and active, its relationship with the CEO tends to be highly contentious and full of potential for friction. Nonprofit CEOs complain that their board "meddles." The directors, in turn, complain that management "usurps" the board's function. This has forced an increasing number of nonprofits to realize that neither board nor CEO is "the boss." They are colleagues, working for the same goal but each having a different task. And they have learned that it is the CEO's responsibility to define the tasks of each, the board's and his or her own.

For example, a large electric co-op in the Pacific Northwest created ten board committees, one for every member. Each has a specific work assignment: community relations, electricity rates, personnel, service standards, and so on. Together with the coop's volunteer chairman and its paid CEO, each of these one-person committees defines its one-year and three-year objectives and the work needed to attain them, which usually requires five to eight days a year from the board member. The chairman reviews each member's work and performance every year, and a member whose performance is found wanting two years in a row cannot stand for reelection. In addition, the chairman, together with three other board members, annually reviews the performance of the entire board and of the CEO.

The key to making a board effective, as this example suggests, is not to talk about its function but to organize its work. More and more nonprofits are doing just that, among them half a dozen fair-sized liberal arts colleges, a leading theological seminary, and some large research hospitals and museums. Ironically, these approaches reinvent the way the first nonprofit board in America was set up 300 years ago: the Harvard University Board of Overseers. Each member is assigned as a "visitor" to one area in the university—the Medical School, the Astronomy Department, the investment of the endowment—and acts both as a source of knowledge to that area and as a critic of its performance. It is a common saying in American academia that Harvard has the only board that makes a difference.

The weakening of the large corporation's board would, many of us predicted (beginning with Myles Mace), weaken management rather than strengthen it. It would diffuse management's accountability for performance and results; and indeed, it is the rare big-company board that reviews the CEO's performance against preset business objectives. Weakening the board would also, we predicted, deprive top management of effective and credible support if it were attacked. These predictions have been borne out amply in the recent rash of hostile takeovers.

To restore management's ability to manage we will have to make boards effective again—and that should be considered a responsibility of the CEO. A few first steps have been taken. The audit committee in most companies now has a real rather than a make-believe job responsibility. A few companies—though so far almost no large ones—have a small board committee on succession and executive development, which regularly meets with senior executives to discuss their performance and their plans. But I know of no company so far where there are work plans for the board and any kind of review of the board's performance. And few do what the larger nonprofits now do routinely: put a new board member through systematic training.

Nonprofits used to say, "We don't pay volunteers so we cannot make demands upon them." Now they are more likely to say, "Volunteers must get far greater satisfaction from their accomplishments and make a greater contribution precisely because they do not get a paycheck." The steady transformation of the volunteer from well-meaning amateur to trained, professional, unpaid staff member is the most significant development in the nonprofit sector—as well as the one with the most far-reaching implications for tomorrow's businesses.

A Midwestern Catholic diocese may have come furthest in this process. It now has fewer than half the priests and nuns it had only 15 years ago. Yet it has greatly expanded its activities—in some cases, such as help for the homeless and for drug abusers, more than doubling them. It still has many traditional volunteers like the Altar Guild members who arrange flowers. But now it is also being served by some 2,000 part-time unpaid staff who run the Catholic charities, perform administrative jobs in parochial schools, and organize youth activities, college Newman Clubs, and even some retreats.

A similar change has taken place at the First Baptist Church in Richmond, Virginia, one of the largest and oldest churches in the Southern Baptist Convention. When Dr. Peter James Flamming took over five years ago, the church had been going downhill for many years, as is typical of old, inner-city churches. Today it again has 4,000 communicants and runs a dozen community outreach programs as well as a full complement of in-church ministries. The church has only nine paid full-time employees. But of its 4,000 communicants, 1,000 serve as unpaid staff.

This development is by no means confined to religious organizations. The American Heart Association has chapters in every city of any size throughout the country. Yet its paid staff is limited to those at national headquarters, with just a few traveling troubleshooters serving the field. Volunteers manage and staff the chapters, with full responsibility for community health education as well as fund raising.

These changes are, in part, a response to need. With close to half the adult population already serving as volunteers, their overall number is unlikely to grow. And with money always in short supply, the nonprofits cannot add paid staff. If they want to add to their activities—and needs are growing—they have to make volunteers more productive, have to give them more work and more responsibility. But the major impetus for the change in the volunteer's role has come from the volunteers themselves.

More and more volunteers are educated people in managerial or professional jobs—some preretirement men and women in their fifties, even more baby-boomers who are reaching their mid-thirties or forties. These people are not satisfied with being helpers. They are knowledge workers in the jobs in which they earn their living, and they want to be knowledge workers in the jobs in which they contribute to society—that is, their volunteer work. If nonprofit organizations want to attract and hold them, they have to put their competence and knowledge to work. They have to offer meaningful achievement.

Many nonprofits systematically recruit for such people. Seasoned volunteers are assigned to scan the newcomers—the new member in a church or synagogue, the neighbor who collects for the Red Cross—to find those with leadership talent and persuade them to try themselves in more demanding assignments. Then senior staff (either a full-timer on the payroll or a seasoned volunteer) interviews the newcomers to assess their strengths and place them accordingly. Volunteers may also be assigned both a mentor and a supervisor with whom they work out their performance goals. These advisers are two different people, as a rule, and both, ordinarily, volunteers themselves.

The Girl Scouts, which employs 730,000 volunteers and only 6,000 paid staff for 3-1/2 million girl members, works this way. A volunteer typically starts by driving youngsters once a week to a meeting. Then a more seasoned volunteer draws her into other work—accompanying Girl Scouts selling cookies door-to-door, assisting a Brownie leader on a camping trip. Out of this step-by-step process evolve the volunteer boards of the local councils and, eventually, the Girl Scouts governing organ, the National Board. Each step, even the very first, has its own compulsory training program, usually conducted by a woman who is herself a volunteer. Each has specific performance standards and performance goals.

What do these unpaid staff people themselves demand? What makes them stay—and, of course, they can leave at any time. Their first and most important demand is that the nonprofit have a clear mission, one that drives everything the organization does. A senior vice president in a large regional bank has two small children. Yet she just took over as chair of the state chapter of Nature Conservancy, which finds, buys, and manages endangered natural ecologies. "I love my job," she said, when I asked her why she took on such heavy additional work, "and of course the bank has a creed. But it doesn't really know what it contributes. At Nature Conservancy, I know what I am here for."

The second thing this new breed requires, indeed demands, is training, training, and more training. And, in turn, the most effective way to motivate and hold veterans is to recognize their expertise and use them to train newcomers. Then these knowledge workers demand responsibility—above all, for thinking through and setting their own performance goals. They expect to be consulted and to participate in making decisions that affect their work and the work of the organization as a whole. And they expect opportunities for advancement, that is, a chance to take on more demanding assignments and more responsibility as their performance warrants. That is why a good many nonprofits have developed career ladders for their volunteers.

Supporting all this activity is accountability. Many of today's knowledge-worker volunteers insist on having their performance reviewed against preset objectives at least once a year. And increasingly, they expect their organizations to remove nonperformers by moving them to other assignments that better fit their capacities or by counseling them to leave. "It's worse than the Marine Corps boot camp," says the priest in charge of volunteers in the Midwestern diocese, "but we have 400 people on the waiting list." One large and growing Midwestern art museum requires of its volunteers— board members, fundraisers, docents, and the people who edit the museum's newsletter—that they set their goals each year, appraise themselves against these goals each year, and resign when they fail to meet their goals two years in a row. So does a fair-sized Jewish organization working on college campuses.

These volunteer professionals are still a minority, but a significant one—perhaps a tenth of the total volunteer population. And they are growing in numbers and, more important, in their impact on the nonprofit sector. Increasingly, nonprofits say what the minister in a large pastoral church says: "There is no laity in this church; there are only pastors, a few paid, most unpaid."

This move from nonprofit volunteer to unpaid professional may be the most important development in American society today. We hear a great deal about the decay and dissolution of family and community and about the loss of values. And, of course, there is reason for concern. But the nonprofits are generating a powerful countercurrent. They are forging new bonds of community, a new commitment to active citizenship, to social responsibility, to values. And surely what the nonprofit contributes to the volunteer is as important as what the volunteer contributes to the nonprofit. Indeed, it may be fully as important as the service, whether religious, educational, or welfare related, that the nonprofit provides in the community.

This development also carries a clear lesson for business. Managing the knowledge worker for productivity is the challenge ahead for American management. The nonprofits are showing us how to do that. It requires a clear mission, careful placement and continuous learning and teaching, management by objectives and self-control, high demands but corresponding responsibility, and accountability for performance and results.

There is also, however, a clear warning to American business in this transformation of volunteer work. The students in the program for senior and middle-level executives in which I teach work in a wide diversity of businesses: banks and insurance companies, large retail chains, aerospace and computer companies, real estate developers, and many others. But most of them also serve as volunteers in nonprofits—in a church, on the board of the college they graduated from, as scout leaders, with the YMCA or the Community Chest or the local symphony orchestra. When I ask them why they do it, far too many give the same answer: Because in my job there isn't much challenge, not enough achievement, not enough responsibility; and there is no mission, there is only expediency.

Originally published in July–August 1989. Reprint 89404

Note

1. A good example is Myles Mace, "The President and the Board of Directors," HBR March–April 1972, p. 37.

The New Society of Organizations

EVERY FEW HUNDRED YEARS throughout Western history, a sharp transformation has occurred. In a matter of decades, society altogether rearranges itself—its world view, its basic values, its social and political structures, its arts, its key institutions. Fifty years later a new world exists. And the people born into that world cannot even imagine the world in which their grandparents lived and into which their own parents were born.

Our age is such a period of transformation. Only this time the transformation is not confined to Western society and Western history. Indeed, one of the fundamental changes is that there is no longer a "Western" history or a "Western" civilization. There is only world history and world civilization.

Whether this transformation began with the emergence of the first non-Western country, Japan, as a great economic power or with the first computer—that is, with information—is moot. My own candidate would be the GI Bill of Rights, which gave every American soldier returning from World War II the money to attend a university, something that would have made absolutely no sense only 30 years earlier at the end of World War I. The GI Bill of Rights and the enthusiastic response to it on the part of America's veterans signaled the shift to a knowledge society.

In this society, knowledge is *the* primary resource for individuals and for the economy overall. Land, labor, and capital—the economist's traditional factors of production—do not disappear, but they become secondary. They can be obtained, and obtained easily, provided there is specialized knowledge. At the same time, however, specialized knowledge by itself produces nothing. It can become productive only when it is integrated into a task. And that is why the knowledge society is also a society of organizations: the purpose and function of every organization, business and non-business alike, is the integration of specialized knowledges into a common task.

If history is any guide, this transformation will not be completed until 2010 or 2020. Therefore, it is risky to try to foresee in every detail the world that is emerging. But what new questions will arise and where the big issues will lie we can, I believe, already discover with a high degree of probability.

In particular, we already know the central tensions and issues that confront the society of organizations: the tension created by the community's need for stability and the organization's need to destabilize; the relationship between individual and organization and the responsibilities of one to another; the tension that arises from the organization's need for autonomy and society's stake in the Common Good; the rising demand for socially responsible organizations; the tension between specialists with specialized knowledges and performance as a team. All of these will be central concerns, especially in the developed world, for years to come. They will not be resolved by pronunciamento or philosophy or legislation. They will be resolved where they originate: in the individual organization and in the manager's office.

Society, community, and family are all conserving institutions. They try to maintain stability and to prevent, or at least to slow, change. But the modern organization is a destabilizer. It must be organized for innovation and innovation, as the great Austro-American economist Joseph Schumpeter said, is "creative destruction." And it must be organized for the systematic abandonment of whatever is

Idea in Brief

Managers in every organization from the largest publicly owned company to the smallest not-for-profit face the same unsettling imperative: to build the change into their organization's very structure. On the one hand, this means being prepared to abandon everything that the organization does. On the other, it means constantly creating the new. Unless this process of abandonment and creation goes on without ceasing, the organization will very soon find itself obsolescent—losing performance and with it the ability to attract and hold the people on whom its performance depends.

What drives this imperative is the nature of the organization itself. Every organization exists to put knowledge to work, but knowledge changes fast, with today's certainties becoming tomorrow's absurdities. That is why any knowledgeable individual must likewise acquire new knowledge every several years or also become "obsolete."

Familiar as the term "organization" is, we have only begun to reckon with the implications of living in a world in which the fundamental unit of society is—and must be—destabilizing. That is why questions of social responsibility now arise so often and from so many quarters. We need new ways to understand the relationship between organizations and their employees, who may in fact be unpaid volunteers, independent professionals whose organization is a network, or knowledgeable specialists who can—and often do—move on at any moment.

For more than 600 years, no society has had as many competing centers of power as the one in which we now live. Drucker explains why change is—and must be—the only constant in an organization's life and explores the consequences for managers, individuals, and society overall.

established, customary, familiar, and comfortable, whether that is a product, service, or process; a set of skills; human and social relationships; or the organization itself. In short, it must be organized for constant change. The organization's function is to put knowledge to work—on tools, products, and processes; on the design of work; on knowledge itself. It is the nature of knowledge that it changes fast and that today's certainties always become tomorrow's absurdities.

Skills change slowly and infrequently. If an ancient Greek stonecutter came back to life today and went to work in a stone mason's yard, the only change of significance would be the design he was asked to carve on the tombstones. The tools he would use are the same, only now they have electric batteries in the handles. Throughout history, the craftsman who had learned a trade after five or seven years of apprenticeship had learned, by age eighteen or nineteen, everything he would ever need to use during his lifetime. In the society of organizations, however, it is safe to assume that anyone with any knowledge will have to acquire new knowledge every four or five years or become obsolete.

This is doubly important because the changes that affect a body of knowledge most profoundly do not, as a rule, come out of its own domain. After Gutenberg first used movable type, there was practically no change in the craft of printing for 400 years—until the steam engine came in. The greatest challenge to the railroad came not from changes in railroading but from the automobile, the truck, and the airplane. The pharmaceutical industry is being profoundly changed today by knowledge coming from genetics and microbiology, disciplines that few biologists had heard of 40 years ago.

And it is by no means only science or technology that creates new knowledge and makes old knowledge obsolete. Social innovation is equally important and often more important than scientific innovation. Indeed, what triggered the present worldwide crisis in that proudest of nineteenth-century institutions, the commercial bank, was not the computer or any other technological change. It was the discovery by nonbankers that an old but hitherto rather obscure financial instrument, commercial paper, could be used to finance companies and would thus deprive the banks of the business on which they had held a monopoly for 200 years and which gave them most of their income: the commercial loan. The greatest change of all is probably that in the last 40 years purposeful innovation—both technical and social—has itself become an organized discipline that is both teachable and learnable.

Nor is rapid knowledge-based change confined to business, as many still believe. No organization in the 50 years since World War II has changed more than the U.S. military. Uniforms have remained the same. Titles of rank have remained the same. But weapons have changed completely, as the Gulf War of 1991 dramatically demonstrated; military doctrines and concepts have changed even more drastically, as have the armed services' organizational structures, command structures, relationships, and responsibilities.

Similarly, it is a safe prediction that in the next 50 years, schools and universities will change more and more drastically than they have since they assumed their present form more than 300 years ago when they reorganized themselves around the printed book. What will force these changes is, in part, new technology, such as computers, videos, and telecasts via satellite; in part the demands of a knowledge-based society in which organized learning must become a lifelong process for knowledge workers; and in part new theory about how human beings learn.

For managers, the dynamics of knowledge impose one clear imperative: every organization has to build the management of change into its very structure.

On the one hand, this means every organization has to prepare for the abandonment of everything it does. Managers have to learn to ask every few years of every process, every product, every procedure, every policy: "If we did not do this already, would we go into it now knowing what we now know?" If the answer is no, the organization has to ask, "So what do we do now?" And it has to *do* something, and not say, "Let's make another study." Indeed, organizations increasingly will have to *plan* abandonment rather than try to prolong the life of a successful product, policy, or practice—something that so far only a few large Japanese companies have faced up to.

On the other hand, every organization must devote itself to creating the new. Specifically, every management has to draw on three systematic practices. The first is continuing improvement of everything the organization does, the process the Japanese call *kaizen*. Every artist throughout history has practiced kaizen, or organized, continuous self-improvement. But so far only the Japanese— perhaps because of their Zen tradition—have embodied it in the daily life and work of their business organizations (although not in their singularly change-resistant universities). The aim of kaizen is to improve a product or service so that it becomes a truly different product or service in two or three years' time.

Second, every organization will have to learn to exploit its knowledge, that is, to develop the next generation of applications from its own successes. Again, Japanese businesses have done the best with this endeavor so far, as demonstrated by the success of the consumer electronics manufacturers in developing one new product after another from the same American invention, the tape recorder. But successful exploitation of their successes is also one of the strengths of the fast-growing American pastoral churches.

Finally, every organization will have to learn to innovate—and innovation can now be organized and must be organized—as a systematic process. And then, of course, one comes back to abandonment, and the process starts all over. Unless this is done, the knowledge-based organization will very soon find itself obsolescent, losing performance capacity and with it the ability to attract and hold the skilled and knowledgeable people on whom its performance depends.

The need to organize for change also requires a high degree of decentralization. That is because the organization must be structured to make decisions quickly. And those decisions must be based on closeness—to performance, to the market, to technology, and to all the many changes in society, the environment, demographics, and knowledge that provide opportunities for innovation if they are seen and utilized.

All this implies, however, that the organizations of the post-capitalist society must constantly upset, disorganize, and destabilize the community. They must change the demand for skills and knowledges: just when every technical university is geared up to teach physics, organizations need geneticists. Just when bank employees are most proficient in credit analysis, they will need to be investment counselors. But also, businesses must be free to close factories on which local communities depend for employment or to replace grizzled model makers who have spent years learning their craft with 25-year-old whiz kids who know computer simulation.

Similarly, hospitals must be able to move the delivery of babies into a free-standing birthing center when the knowledge base and technology of obstetrics change. And we must be able to close a hospital altogether when changes in medical knowledge, technology, and practice make a hospital with fewer than 200 beds both uneconomical and incapable of giving first-rate care. For a hospital—or a school or any other community organization—to discharge its social function we must be able to close it down, no matter how deeply rooted in the local community it is and how much beloved, if changes in demographics, technology, or knowledge set new prerequisites for performance.

But every one of such changes upsets the community, disrupts it, deprives it of continuity. Every one is "unfair." Every one destabilizes.

Equally disruptive is another fact of organizational life: the modern organization must be *in* a community but cannot be *of* it. An organization's members live in a particular place, speak its language, send their children to its schools, vote, pay taxes, and need to feel at home there. Yet the organization cannot submerge itself in the community nor subordinate itself to the community's ends. Its "culture" has to transcend community.

It is the nature of the task, not the community in which the task is being performed, that determines the culture of an organization. The American civil servant, though totally opposed to communism, will understand immediately what a Chinese colleague tells him about bureaucratic intrigues in Beijing. But he would be totally baffled in his own Washington, D.C. if he were to sit in on a discussion of the next week's advertising promotions by the managers of the local grocery chain.

To perform its task the organization has to be organized and managed the same way as others of its type. For example, we hear a great deal about the differences in management between Japanese and American companies. But a large Japanese company functions very much like a large American company; and both function very much like a large German or British company. Likewise, no one will ever doubt that he or she is in a hospital, no matter where the hospital is located. The same holds true for schools and universities, for labor unions and research labs, for museums and opera houses, for astronomical observatories and large farms.

In addition, each organization has a value system that is determined by its task. In every hospital in the world, health care is considered the ultimate good. In every school in the world, learning is considered the ultimate good. In every business in the world, production and distribution of goods or services is considered the ultimate good. For the organization to perform to a high standard, its members must believe that what it is doing is, in the last analysis, the one contribution to community and society on which all others depend.

In its culture, therefore, the organization will always transcend the community. If an organization's culture and the values of its community clash, the organization must prevail—or else it will not make its social contribution. "Knowledge knows no boundaries," says an old proverb. There has been a "town and gown" conflict ever since the first university was established more than 750 years ago. But such a conflict—between the autonomy the organization needs in order to perform and the claims of the community, between the values of the organization and those of the community, between the decisions facing the organization and the interests of the community—is inherent in the society of organizations.

_____

The issue of social responsibility is also inherent in the society of organizations. The modern organization has and must have social power—and a good deal of it. It needs power to make decisions about people: whom to hire, whom to fire, whom to promote. It needs power to establish the rules and disciplines required to produce results: for example, the assignment of jobs and tasks and the establishment of working hours. It needs power to decide which factories to build where and which factories to close. It needs power to set prices, and so on.

And nonbusinesses have the greatest social power—far more, in fact, than business enterprises. Few organizations in history were ever granted the power the university has today. Refusing to admit a student or to grant a student the diploma is tantamount to debarring that person from careers and opportunities. Similarly, the power of the American hospital to deny a physician admitting privileges is the power to exclude that physician from the practice of medicine. The labor union's power over admission to apprenticeship or its control of access to employment in a "closed shop," where only union members can be hired, gives the union tremendous social power.

The power of the organization can be restrained by political power. It can be made subject to due process and to review by the courts. But it must be exercised by individual organizations rather than by political authorities. This is why postcapitalist society talks so much about social responsibilities of the organization.

It is futile to argue, as Milton Friedman, the American economist and Noble-laureate does, that a business has only one responsibility: economic performance. Economic performance is the *first* responsibility of a business. Indeed, a business that does not show a profit at least equal to its cost of capital is irresponsible; it wastes society's resources. Economic performance is the base without which a business cannot discharge any other responsibilities, cannot be a good employee, a good citizen, a good neighbor. But economic performance is not the *only* responsibility of a business any more than educational performance is the only responsibility of a school or health care the only responsibility of a hospital.

Unless power is balanced by responsibility, it becomes tyranny. Furthermore, without responsibility power always degenerates into nonperformance, and organizations must perform. So the demand for socially responsible organizations will not go away but rather widen.

Fortunately, we also know, if only in rough outline, how to answer the problem of social responsibility. Every organization must assume full responsibility for its impact on employees, the environment, customers, and whomever and whatever it touches. That is its social responsibility. But we also know that society will increasingly look to major organizations, for-profit and nonprofit alike, to tackle major social ills. And there we had better be watchful because good intentions are not always socially responsible. It is irresponsible for an organization to accept—let alone to pursue—responsibilities that would impede its capacity to perform its main task and mission or to act where it has no competence.

Organization has become an everyday term. Everybody nods when somebody says, "In our organization, everything should revolve around the customer" or "In this organization, they never forget a mistake." And most, if not all, social tasks in every developed country are performed in and by an organization of one kind or another. Yet no one in the United States—or anyplace else—talked of "organizations" until after World War II. *The Concise Oxford Dictionary* did not even list the term in its current meaning in the 1950 edition. It is only the emergence of management since World War II, what I call the "Management Revolution," that has allowed us to see that the organization is discrete and distinct from society's other institutions.

Unlike "community," "society," or "family," organizations are purposefully designed and always specialized. Community and society are defined by the bonds that hold their members together, whether they be language, culture, history, or locality. An organization is defined by its task. The symphony orchestra does not attempt to cure the sick; it plays music. The hospital takes care of the sick but does not attempt to play Beethoven.

Indeed, an organization is effective only if it concentrates on one task. Diversification destroys the performance capacity of an organization, whether it is a business, a labor union, a school, a hospital, a community service, or a house of worship. Society and community must be multidimensional; they are environments. An organization is a tool. And as with any other tool, the more specialized it is, the greater its capacity to perform its given task.

Because the modern organization is composed of specialists, each with his or her own narrow area of expertise, its mission must be crystal clear. The organization must be single-minded, or its members will become confused. They will follow their own specialty rather than apply it to the common task. They will each define "results" in terms of their own specialty and impose its values on the organization. Only a focused and common mission will hold the organization together and enable it to produce. Without such a mission, the organization will soon lose credibility and, with it, its ability to attract the very people it needs to perform.

It can be all too easy for managers to forget that joining an organization is always voluntary. De facto there may be little choice. But even where membership is all but compulsory—as membership in the Catholic church was in all the countries of Europe for many centuries for all but a handful of Jews and Gypsies—the fiction of voluntary choice is always carefully maintained: the godfather at the infant's baptism pledges the child's voluntary acceptance of membership in the church.

Likewise, it may be difficult to leave an organization—the Mafia, for instance, a big Japanese company, the Jesuit order. But it is always possible. And the more an organization becomes an organization of knowledge workers, the easier it is to leave it and move elsewhere. Therefore, an organization is always in competition for its most essential resource: qualified, knowledgeable people.

All organizations now say routinely, "People are our greatest asset." Yet few practice what they preach, let alone truly believe it. Most still believe, though perhaps not consciously, what nineteenth-century employers believed: people need us more than we need them. But, in fact, organizations have to market membership as much as they market products and services—and perhaps more. They have to attract people, hold people, recognize and reward people, motivate people, and serve and satisfy people.

The relationship between knowledge workers and their organizations is a distinctly new phenomenon, one for which we have no good term. For example, an employee, by definition, is someone who gets paid for working. Yet the largest single group of "employees" in the United States is comprised of the millions of men and women who work several hours a week without pay for one or another nonprofit organization. They are clearly "staff" and consider themselves as such, but they are unpaid volunteers. Similarly, many people who work as employees are not employed in any legal sense because they do not work for someone else. Fifty or sixty years ago, we would have spoken of these people (many, if not most, of whom are educated professionals) as "independent"; today we speak of the "self-employed."

These discrepancies—and they exist in just about every language—remind us why new realities often demand new words. But until such a word emerges, this is probably the best definition of employees in the post-capitalist society: people whose ability to make a contribution depends on having access to an organization.

As far as the employees who work in subordinate and menial occupations are concerned—the salesclerk in the supermarket, the cleaning woman in the hospital, the delivery-truck driver—the consequences of this new definition are small. For all practical purposes, their position may not be too different from that of the wage earner, the "worker" of yesterday, whose direct descendants they are. In fact, this is precisely one of the central social problems modern society faces.

But the relationship between the organization and knowledge workers, who already number at least one-third and more likely two-fifths of all employees, is radically different, as is that between the organization and volunteers. They can work only because there is an organization, thus they too are dependent. But at the same time, they own the "means of production"—their knowledge. In this respect, they are independent and highly mobile.

Knowledge workers still need the tools of production. In fact, capital investment in the tools of the knowledge employee may already be higher than the capital investment in the tools of the manufacturing worker ever was. (And the social investment, for example, the investment in a knowledge worker's education, is many times the investment in the manual worker's education.) But this capital investment is unproductive unless the knowledge worker brings to bear on it the knowledge that he or she owns and that cannot be taken away. Machine operators in the factory did as they were told. The machine decided not only what to do but how to do it. The knowledge employee may well need a machine, whether it be a computer, an ultrasound analyzer, or a telescope. But the machine will not tell the knowledge worker what to do, let alone how to do it. And without this knowledge, which belongs to the employee, the machine is unproductive.

Further, machine operators, like all workers throughout history, could be told what to do, how to do it, and how fast to do it. Knowledge workers cannot be supervised effectively. Unless they know more about their specialty than anybody else in the organization, they are basically useless. The marketing manager may tell the market researcher what the company needs to know about the design of a new product and the market segment in which it should be positioned. But it is the market researcher's job to tell the president of the company what market research is needed, how to set it up, and what the results mean.

During the traumatic restructuring of American business in the 1980s, thousands, if not hundreds of thousands, of knowledge employees lost their jobs. Their companies were acquired, merged, spun off, or liquidated. Yet within a few months, most of them found new jobs in which to put their knowledge to work. The transition period was painful, and in about half the cases, the new job did not pay quite as much as the old one did and may not have been as enjoyable. But the laid-off technicians, professionals, and managers found they had the "capital," the knowledge: they owned the means of production. Somebody else, the organization, had the tools of production. The two needed each other.

One consequence of this new relationship—and it is another new tension in modern society—is that loyalty can no longer be obtained by the paycheck. The organization must earn loyalty by proving to its knowledge employees that it offers them exceptional opportunities for putting their knowledge to work. Not so long ago we talked about "labor." Increasingly we are talking about "human resources." This change reminds us that it is the individual, and especially the skilled and knowledgeable employee, who decides in large measure what he or she will contribute to the organization and how great the yield from his or her knowledge will be.

———————

Because the modern organization consists of knowledge specialists, it has to be an organization of equals, of colleagues and associates. No knowledge ranks higher than another; each is judged by its contribution to the common task rather than by any inherent superiority or inferiority. Therefore, the modern organization cannot be an organization of boss and subordinate. It must be organized as a team.

There are only three kinds of teams. One is the sort of team that plays together in tennis doubles. In that team—and it has to be small—each member adapts himself or herself to the personality, the skills, the strengths, and the weaknesses of the other member or members. Then there is the team that plays European football or soccer. Each player has a fixed position; but the whole team moves together (except for the goalie) while individual members retain their relative positions. Finally, there is the American baseball team—or the orchestra—in which all the members have fixed positions.

At any given time, an organization can play only one kind of game. And it can use only one kind of team for any given task. Which team to use or game to play is one of the riskiest decisions in the life of an organization. Few things are as difficult in an organization as transforming from one kind of team to another.

Traditionally, American industry used a baseball-style team to produce a new product or model. Research did its work and passed it on to engineering. Engineering did its work and passed it on to manufacturing. Manufacturing did its work and passed it on to marketing. Accounting usually came in at the manufacturing phase. Personnel usually came in only when there was a true crisis—and often not even then.

Then the Japanese reorganized their new product development into a soccer team. In such a team, each function does its own work, but from the beginning they work together. They move with the task, so to speak, the way a soccer team moves with the ball. It took the Japanese at least 15 years to learn how to do this. But once they had mastered the new concept, they cut development time by two-thirds. Where traditionally it has taken 5 years to bring out a new automobile model, Toyota, Nissan, and Honda now do it in 18 months. This, as much as their quality control, has given the Japanese the upper hand in both the American and European automobile markets.

Some American manufacturers have been working hard to reorganize their development work according to the Japanese model. Ford Motor Company, for instance, began to do so in the early 1980s. Ten years later, in the early 1990s, it has made considerable progress—but not nearly enough to catch up with the Japanese. Changing a team demands the most difficult learning imaginable: unlearning. It demands giving up hard-earned skills, habits of a lifetime, deeply cherished values of craftsmanship and professionalism, and—perhaps the most difficult of all—it demands giving up old and treasured human relationships. It means abandoning what people have always considered "our community" or "our family."

But if the organization is to perform, it must be organized as a team. When modern organizations first arose in the closing years of the nineteenth century, the only model was the military. The Prussian Army was as much a marvel of organization for the world of 1870 as Henry Ford's assembly line was for the world of 1920. In the army of 1870, each member did much the same thing, and the number of people with any knowledge was infinitesimally small. The army was organized by command-and-control, and business enterprise as well as most other institutions copied that model. This is now rapidly changing. As more and more organizations become information-based, they are transforming themselves into soccer or tennis teams, that is, into responsibility-based organizations in which every member must act as a responsible decision maker. All members, in other words, have to see themselves as "executives."

Even so, an organization must be managed. The management may be intermittent and perfunctory, as it is, for instance, in the Parent-Teacher Association at a U.S. suburban school. Or management may be a full-time and demanding job for a fairly large group of people, as it is in the military, the business enterprise, the labor union, and the university. But there have to be people who make decisions or nothing will ever get done. There have to be people who are accountable for the organization's mission, its spirit, its performance, its results. Society, community, and family may have "leaders," but only organizations know a "management." And while this management must have considerable authority, its job in the modern organization is not to command. It is to inspire.

The society of organizations is unprecedented in human history. It is unprecedented in its performance capacity both because each of its constituent organizations is a highly specialized tool designed for one specific task and because each bases itself on the organization and deployment of knowledge. It is unprecedented in its structure. But it is also unprecedented in its tensions and problems. Not all of these are serious. In fact, some of them we already know how to resolve—issues of social responsibility, for example. But there are other areas where we do not know the right answer and where we may not even be asking the right questions yet.

There is, for instance, the tension between the community's need for continuity and stability and the organization's need to be an innovator and destabilizer. There is the split between "literati" and "managers." Both are needed: the former to produce knowledge, the latter to apply knowledge and make it productive. But the former focus on words and ideas, the latter on people, work, and performance. There is the threat to the very basis of the society of organizations— the knowledge base—that arises from ever greater specialization, from the shift from knowledge to *knowledges*. But the greatest and most difficult challenge is that presented by society's new pluralism.

For more than 600 years, no society has had as many centers of power as the society in which we now live. The Middle Ages indeed knew pluralism. Society was composed of hundreds of competing and autonomous power centers: feudal lords and knights, exempt bishoprics, autonomous monasteries, "free" cities. In some places, the Austrian Tyrol, for example, there were even "free peasants," beholden to no one but the Emperor. There were also autonomous craft guilds and transnational trading leagues like the Hanseatic Merchants and the merchant bankers of Florence, toll and tax collectors, local "parliaments" with legislative and tax-raising powers, private armies available for hire, and myriads more.

Modern history in Europe—and equally in Japan—has been the history of the subjugation of all competing centers of power by one central authority, first called the "prince," then the "state." By the middle of the nineteenth century, the unitary state had triumphed in every developed country except the United States, which remained profoundly pluralistic in its religious and educational organizations. Indeed, the abolition of pluralism was the "progressive" cause for nearly 600 years.

But just when the triumph of the state seemed assured, the first new organization arose—the large business enterprise. (This, of course, always happens when the "End of History" is announced.) Since then, one new organization after another has sprung up. And old organizations like the university, which in Europe seemed to have been brought safely under the control of central governments, have become autonomous again. Ironically, twentieth-century totalitarianism, especially communism, represented the last desperate attempt to save the old progressive creed in which there is only one center of power and one organization rather than a pluralism of competing and autonomous organizations.

That attempt failed, as we know. But the failure of central authority, in and of itself, does nothing to address the issues that follow from a pluralistic society. To illustrate, consider a story that many people have heard or, more accurately, misheard.

During his lifetime, Charles E. Wilson was a prominent personality in the United States, first as president and chief executive officer of General Motors, at that time the world's largest and most successful manufacturer, then as secretary of defense in the Eisenhower administration. But if Wilson is remembered at all today it is for something he did *not* say: "What is good for General Motors is good for the United States." What Wilson actually said in his 1953 confirmation hearings for the Defense Department job was: "What is good for the United States is good for General Motors."

Wilson tried for the remainder of his life to correct the misquote. But no one listened to him. Everyone argued, "If he didn't say it, he surely believes it—in fact he *should* believe it." For as has been said, executives in an organization—whether business or university or hospital or the Boy Scouts—must believe that its mission and task are society's most important mission and task as well as the foundation for everything else. If they do not believe this, their organization will soon lose faith in itself, self-confidence, pride, and the ability to perform.

The diversity that is characteristic of a developed society and that provides its great strength is only possible because of the specialized, single-task organizations that we have developed since the Industrial Revolution and, especially, during the last 50 years. But the feature that gives them the capacity to perform is precisely that each is autonomous and specialized, informed only by its own narrow mission and vision, its own narrow values, and not by any consideration of society and community.

Therefore, we come back to the old—and never resolved—problem of the pluralistic society: Who takes care of the Common Good? Who defines it? Who balances the separate and often competing goals and values of society's institutions? Who makes the trade-off decisions and on what basis should they be made?

Medieval feudalism was replaced by the unitary sovereign state precisely because it could not answer these questions. But the unitary sovereign state has now itself been replaced by a new pluralism—a pluralism of function rather than one of political power—because it could neither satisfy the needs of society nor perform the necessary tasks of community. That, in the final analysis, is the most fundamental lesson to be learned from the failure of socialism, the failure of the belief in the all-embracing and all-powerful state. The challenge that faces us now, and especially in the developed, free-market democracies such as the United States, is to make the pluralism of autonomous, knowledge-based organizations redound both to economic performance and to political and social cohesion.

Originally published in September–October 1992. Reprint 92503

Managing
Oneself

HISTORY'S GREAT ACHIEVERS—a Napoléon, a da Vinci, a Mozart—have always managed themselves. That, in large measure, is what makes them great achievers. But they are rare exceptions, so unusual both in their talents and their accomplishments as to be considered outside the boundaries of ordinary human existence. Now, most of us, even those of us with modest endowments, will have to learn to manage ourselves. We will have to learn to develop ourselves. We will have to place ourselves where we can make the greatest contribution. And we will have to stay mentally alert and engaged during a 50-year working life, which means knowing how and when to change the work we do.

What Are My Strengths?

Most people think they know what they are good at. They are usually wrong. More often, people know what they are not good at—and even then more people are wrong than right. And yet, a person can perform only from strength. One cannot build performance on weaknesses, let alone on something one cannot do at all.

Throughout history, people had little need to know their strengths. A person was born into a position and a line of work: The peasant's son would also be a peasant; the artisan's daughter, an artisan's wife; and so on. But now people have choices. We need to know our strengths in order to know where we belong.

The only way to discover your strengths is through feedback analysis. Whenever you make a key decision or take a key action, write down what you expect will happen. Nine or 12 months later, compare the actual results with your expectations. I have been practicing this method for 15 to 20 years now, and every time I do it, I am surprised. The feedback analysis showed me, for instance—and to my great surprise—that I have an intuitive understanding of technical people, whether they are engineers or accountants or market researchers. It also showed me that I don't really resonate with generalists.

Feedback analysis is by no means new. It was invented sometime in the fourteenth century by an otherwise totally obscure German theologian and picked up quite independently, some 150 years later, by John Calvin and Ignatius of Loyola, each of whom incorporated it into the practice of his followers. In fact, the steadfast focus on performance and results that this habit produces explains why the institutions these two men founded, the Calvinist church and the Jesuit order, came to dominate Europe within 30 years.

Practiced consistently, this simple method will show you within a fairly short period of time, maybe two or three years, where your strengths lie—and this is the most important thing to know. The method will show you what you are doing or failing to do that deprives you of the full benefits of your strengths. It will show you where you are not particularly competent. And finally, it will show you where you have no strengths and cannot perform.

Several implications for action follow from feedback analysis. First and foremost, concentrate on your strengths. Put yourself where your strengths can produce results.

Second, work on improving your strengths. Analysis will rapidly show where you need to improve skills or acquire new ones. It will also show the gaps in your knowledge—and those can usually be filled. Mathematicians are born, but everyone can learn trigonometry.

Third, discover where your intellectual arrogance is causing disabling ignorance and overcome it. Far too many people—especially people with great expertise in one area—are contemptuous of

Idea in Brief

We live in an age of unprecedented opportunity: If you've got ambition, drive, and smarts, you can rise to the top of your chosen profession—regardless of where you started out. But with opportunity comes responsibility. Companies today aren't managing their knowledge workers' careers. Rather, we must each be our own chief executive officer.

Simply put, it's up to you to carve out your place in the work world and know when to change course. And it's up to you to keep yourself engaged and productive during a work life that may span some 50 years.

To do all of these things well, you'll need to cultivate a deep understanding of yourself. What are your most valuable strengths and most dangerous weaknesses? Equally important, how do you learn and work with others? What are your most deeply held values? And in what type of work environment can you make the greatest contribution?

The implication is clear: Only when you operate from a combination of your strengths and self-knowledge can you achieve true—and lasting—excellence.

knowledge in other areas or believe that being bright is a substitute for knowledge. First-rate engineers, for instance, tend to take pride in not knowing anything about people. Human beings, they believe, are much too disorderly for the good engineering mind. Human resources professionals, by contrast, often pride themselves on their ignorance of elementary accounting or of quantitative methods altogether. But taking pride in such ignorance is self-defeating. Go to work on acquiring the skills and knowledge you need to fully realize your strengths.

It is equally essential to remedy your bad habits—the things you do or fail to do that inhibit your effectiveness and performance. Such habits will quickly show up in the feedback. For example, a planner may find that his beautiful plans fail because he does not follow through on them. Like so many brilliant people, he believes that ideas move mountains. But bulldozers move mountains; ideas show where the bulldozers should go to work. This planner will have to learn that the work does not stop when the plan is completed.

Idea in Practice

To build a life of excellence, begin by asking yourself these questions:

"What are my strengths?"

To accurately identify your strengths, use **feedback analysis**. Every time you make a key decision, write down the outcome you expect. Several months later, compare the actual results with your expected results. Look for patterns in what you're seeing: What results are you skilled at generating? What abilities do you need to enhance in order to get the results you want? What unproductive habits are preventing you from creating the outcomes you

desire? In identifying opportunities for improvement, don't waste time cultivating skill areas where you have little competence. Instead, concentrate on—and build on— your strengths.

"How do I work?"

In what ways do you work best? Do you process information most effectively by reading it, or by hearing others discuss it? Do you accomplish the most by working with other people, or by working alone? Do you perform best while making decisions, or while advising others on key matters? Are you in top form when things

He must find people to carry out the plan and explain it to them. He must adapt and change it as he puts it into action. And finally, he must decide when to stop pushing the plan.

At the same time, feedback will also reveal when the problem is a lack of manners. Manners are the lubricating oil of an organization. It is a law of nature that two moving bodies in contact with each other create friction. This is as true for human beings as it is for inanimate objects. Manners—simple things like saying "please" and "thank you" and knowing a person's name or asking after her family—enable two people to work together whether they like each other or not. Bright people, especially bright young people, often do not understand this. If analysis shows that someone's brilliant work fails again and again as soon as cooperation from others is required, it probably indicates a lack of courtesy—that is, a lack of manners.

Comparing your expectations with your results also indicates what not to do. We all have a vast number of areas in which we have no talent or skill and little chance of becoming even mediocre. In get stressful, or do you function optimally in a highly predictable environment?

"What are my values?"

What are your ethics? What do you see as your most important responsibilities for living a worthy, ethical life? Do your organization's ethics resonate with your own values? If not, your career will likely be marked by frustration and poor performance.

"Where do I belong?"

Consider your strengths, preferred work style, and values. Based on these qualities, in what kind of work environment would you fit in best? Find the perfect fit, and you'll transform yourself from a merely acceptable employee into a star performer.

"What can I contribute?"

In earlier eras, companies told businesspeople what their contribution should be. Today, you have choices. To decide how you can best enhance your organization's performance, first ask what the situation requires. Based on your strengths, work style, and values, how might you make the greatest contribution to your organization's efforts?

those areas a person—and especially a knowledge worker—should not take on work, jobs, and assignments. One should waste as little effort as possible on improving areas of low competence. It takes far more energy and work to improve from incompetence to mediocrity than it takes to improve from first-rate performance to excellence. And yet most people—especially most teachers and most organizations—concentrate on making incompetent performers into mediocre ones. Energy, resources, and time should go instead to making a competent person into a star performer.

How Do I Perform?

Amazingly few people know how they get things done. Indeed, most of us do not even know that different people work and perform differently. Too many people work in ways that are not their ways, and that almost guarantees nonperformance. For knowledge workers, How do I perform? may be an even more important question than What are my strengths?

Like one's strengths, how one performs is unique. It is a matter of personality. Whether personality be a matter of nature or nurture, it surely is formed long before a person goes to work. And *how* a person performs is a given, just as *what* a person is good at or not good at is a given. A person's way of performing can be slightly modified, but it is unlikely to be completely changed—and certainly not easily. Just as people achieve results by doing what they are good at, they also achieve results by working in ways that they best perform. A few common personality traits usually determine how a person performs.

Am I a reader or a listener?

The first thing to know is whether you are a reader or a listener. Far too few people even know that there are readers and listeners and that people are rarely both. Even fewer know which of the two they themselves are. But some examples will show how damaging such ignorance can be.

When Dwight Eisenhower was Supreme Commander of the Allied forces in Europe, he was the darling of the press. His press conferences were famous for their style—General Eisenhower showed total command of whatever question he was asked, and he was able to describe a situation and explain a policy in two or three beautifully polished and elegant sentences. Ten years later, the same journalists who had been his admirers held President Eisenhower in open contempt. He never addressed the questions, they complained, but rambled on endlessly about something else. And they constantly ridiculed him for butchering the King's English in incoherent and ungrammatical answers.

Eisenhower apparently did not know that he was a reader, not a listener. When he was Supreme Commander in Europe, his aides made sure that every question from the press was presented in writing at least half an hour before a conference was to begin. And then Eisenhower was in total command. When he became president, he succeeded two listeners, Franklin D. Roosevelt and Harry Truman. Both men knew themselves to be listeners and both enjoyed free-for-all press conferences. Eisenhower may have felt that he had to do what his two predecessors had done. As a result, he never even heard the questions journalists asked. And Eisenhower is not even an extreme case of a nonlistener.

A few years later, Lyndon Johnson destroyed his presidency, in large measure, by not knowing that he was a listener. His predecessor, John Kennedy, was a reader who had assembled a brilliant group of writers as his assistants, making sure that they wrote to him before discussing their memos in person. Johnson kept these people on his staff—and they kept on writing. He never, apparently, understood one word of what they wrote. Yet as a senator, Johnson had been superb; for parliamentarians have to be, above all, listeners.

Few listeners can be made, or can make themselves, into competent readers—and vice versa. The listener who tries to be a reader will, therefore, suffer the fate of Lyndon Johnson, whereas the reader who tries to be a listener will suffer the fate of Dwight Eisenhower. They will not perform or achieve.

How do I learn?

The second thing to know about how one performs is to know how one learns. Many first-class writers—Winston Churchill is but one example—do poorly in school. They tend to remember their schooling as pure torture. Yet few of their classmates remember it the same way. They may not have enjoyed the school very much, but the worst they suffered was boredom. The explanation is that writers do not, as a rule, learn by listening and reading. They learn by writing. Because schools do not allow them to learn this way, they get poor grades.

Schools everywhere are organized on the assumption that there is only one right way to learn and that it is the same way for everybody. But to be forced to learn the way a school teaches is sheer hell for students who learn differently. Indeed, there are probably half a dozen different ways to learn.

There are people, like Churchill, who learn by writing. Some people learn by taking copious notes. Beethoven, for example, left behind an enormous number of sketchbooks, yet he said he never actually looked at them when he composed. Asked why he kept them, he is reported to have replied, "If I don't write it down immediately, I forget it right away. If I put it into a sketchbook, I never forget it and I never have to look it up again." Some people learn by doing. Others learn by hearing themselves talk.

A chief executive I know who converted a small and mediocre family business into the leading company in its industry was one of those people who learn by talking. He was in the habit of calling his entire senior staff into his office once a week and then talking at them for two or three hours. He would raise policy issues and argue three different positions on each one. He rarely asked his associates for comments or questions; he simply needed an audience to hear himself talk. That's how he learned. And although he is a fairly extreme case, learning through talking is by no means an unusual method. Successful trial lawyers learn the same way, as do many medical diagnosticians (and so do I).

Of all the important pieces of self-knowledge, understanding how you learn is the easiest to acquire. When I ask people, "How do you learn?" most of them know the answer. But when I ask, "Do you act on this knowledge?" few answer yes. And yet, acting on this knowledge is the key to performance; or rather, *not* acting on this knowledge condemns one to nonperformance.

Am I a reader or a listener? and How do I learn? are the first questions to ask. But they are by no means the only ones. To manage yourself effectively, you also have to ask, Do I work well with people, or am I a loner? And if you do work well with people, you then must ask, In what relationship?

Some people work best as subordinates. General George Patton, the great American military hero of World War II, is a prime example. Patton was America's top troop commander. Yet when he was proposed for an independent command, General George Marshall, the U.S. chief of staff—and probably the most successful picker of men in U.S. history—said, "Patton is the best subordinate the American army has ever produced, but he would be the worst commander."

Some people work best as team members. Others work best alone. Some are exceptionally talented as coaches and mentors; others are simply incompetent as mentors.

Another crucial question is, Do I produce results as a decision maker or as an adviser? A great many people perform best as advisers but cannot take the burden and pressure of making the decision. A good many other people, by contrast, need an adviser to force themselves to think; then they can make decisions and act on them with speed, self-confidence, and courage.

This is a reason, by the way, that the number two person in an organization often fails when promoted to the number one position. The top spot requires a decision maker. Strong decision makers often put somebody they trust into the number two spot as their adviser—and in that position the person is outstanding. But in the number one spot, the same person fails. He or she knows what the decision should be but cannot accept the responsibility of actually making it.

Other important questions to ask include, Do I perform well under stress, or do I need a highly structured and predictable environment? Do I work best in a big organization or a small one? Few people work well in all kinds of environments. Again and again, I have seen people who were very successful in large organizations flounder miserably when they moved into smaller ones. And the reverse is equally true.

The conclusion bears repeating: Do not try to change yourself—you are unlikely to succeed. But work hard to improve the way you perform. And try not to take on work you cannot perform or will only perform poorly.

What Are My Values?

To be able to manage yourself, you finally have to ask, What are my values? This is not a question of ethics. With respect to ethics, the rules are the same for everybody, and the test is a simple one. I call it the "mirror test."

In the early years of this century, the most highly respected diplomat of all the great powers was the German ambassador in London. He was clearly destined for great things—to become his country's foreign minister, at least, if not its federal chancellor. Yet in 1906 he abruptly resigned rather than preside over a dinner given by the diplomatic corps for Edward VII. The king was a notorious womanizer and made it clear what kind of dinner he wanted. The ambassador is reported to have said, "I refuse to see a pimp in the mirror in the morning when I shave."

That is the mirror test. Ethics requires that you ask yourself, What kind of person do I want to see in the mirror in the morning? What is ethical behavior in one kind of organization or situation is ethical behavior in another. But ethics is only part of a value system—especially of an organization's value system.

To work in an organization whose value system is unacceptable or incompatible with one's own condemns a person both to frustration and to nonperformance.

Consider the experience of a highly successful human resources executive whose company was acquired by a bigger organization. After the acquisition, she was promoted to do the kind of work she did best, which included selecting people for important positions. The executive deeply believed that a company should hire people for such positions from the outside only after exhausting all the inside possibilities. But her new company believed in first looking outside "to bring in fresh blood." There is something to be said for both approaches—in my experience, the proper one is to do some of both. They are, however, fundamentally incompatible—not as policies but as values. They bespeak different views of the relationship between organizations and people; different views of the responsibility of an organization to its people and their development; and different views of a person's most important contribution to an enterprise. After several years of frustration, the executive quit—at considerable financial loss. Her values and the values of the organization simply were not compatible.

Similarly, whether a pharmaceutical company tries to obtain results by making constant, small improvements or by achieving occasional, highly expensive, and risky "breakthroughs" is not primarily an economic question. The results of either strategy may be pretty much the same. At bottom, there is a conflict between a value system that sees the company's contribution in terms of helping physicians do better what they already do and a value system that is oriented toward making scientific discoveries.

Whether a business should be run for short-term results or with a focus on the long term is likewise a question of values. Financial analysts believe that businesses can be run for both simultaneously. Successful businesspeople know better. To be sure, every company has to produce short-term results. But in any conflict between short-term results and long-term growth, each company will determine its own priority. This is not primarily a disagreement about economics. It is fundamentally a value conflict regarding the function of a business and the responsibility of management.

Value conflicts are not limited to business organizations. One of the fastest-growing pastoral churches in the United States measures success by the number of new parishioners. Its leadership believes that what matters is how many newcomers join the congregation. The Good Lord will then minister to their spiritual needs or at least to the needs of a sufficient percentage. Another pastoral, evangelical church believes that what matters is people's spiritual growth. The church eases out newcomers who join but do not enter into its spiritual life.

Again, this is not a matter of numbers. At first glance, it appears that the second church grows more slowly. But it retains a far larger proportion of newcomers than the first one does. Its growth, in other words, is more solid. This is also not a theological problem, or only secondarily so. It is a problem about values. In a public debate, one pastor argued, "Unless you first come to church, you will never find the gate to the Kingdom of Heaven."

"No," answered the other. "Until you first look for the gate to the Kingdom of Heaven, you don't belong in church."

Organizations, like people, have values. To be effective in an organization, a person's values must be compatible with the organization's values. They do not need to be the same, but they must be close enough to coexist. Otherwise, the person will not only be frustrated but also will not produce results.

A person's strengths and the way that person performs rarely conflict; the two are complementary. But there is sometimes a conflict between a person's values and his or her strengths. What one does well—even very well and successfully—may not fit with one's value system. In that case, the work may not appear to be worth devoting one's life to (or even a substantial portion thereof).

If I may, allow me to interject a personal note. Many years ago, I too had to decide between my values and what I was doing successfully. I was doing very well as a young investment banker in London in the mid-1930s, and the work clearly fit my strengths. Yet I did not see myself making a contribution as an asset manager. People, I realized, were what I valued, and I saw no point in being the richest man in the cemetery. I had no money and no other job prospects. Despite the continuing Depression, I quit—and it was the right thing to do. Values, in other words, are and should be the ultimate test.

Where Do I Belong?

A small number of people know very early where they belong. Mathematicians, musicians, and cooks, for instance, are usually mathematicians, musicians, and cooks by the time they are four or five years old. Physicians usually decide on their careers in their teens, if not earlier. But most people, especially highly gifted people, do not really know where they belong until they are well past their mid-twenties. By that time, however, they should know the answers to the three questions: What are my strengths? How do I perform? and, What are my values? And then they can and should decide where they belong.

Or rather, they should be able to decide where they do *not* belong. The person who has learned that he or she does not perform well in a big organization should have learned to say no to a position in one. The person who has learned that he or she is not a decision maker should have learned to say no to a decision-making assignment. A General Patton (who probably never learned this himself) should have learned to say no to an independent command.

Equally important, knowing the answer to these questions enables a person to say to an opportunity, an offer, or an assignment, "Yes, I will do that. But this is the way I should be doing it. This is the way it should be structured. This is the way the relationships should be. These are the kind of results you should expect from me, and in this time frame, because this is who I am."

Successful careers are not planned. They develop when people are prepared for opportunities because they know their strengths, their method of work, and their values. Knowing where one belongs can transform an ordinary person—hardworking and competent but otherwise mediocre—into an outstanding performer.

What Should I Contribute?

Throughout history, the great majority of people never had to ask the question, What should I contribute? They were told what to contribute, and their tasks were dictated either by the work itself—as it was for the peasant or artisan—or by a master or a mistress—as it was for domestic servants. And until very recently, it was taken for granted that most people were subordinates who did as they were told. Even in the 1950s and 1960s, the new knowledge workers (the so-called organization men) looked to their company's personnel department to plan their careers.

Then in the late 1960s, no one wanted to be told what to do any longer. Young men and women began to ask, What do *I* want to do? And what they heard was that the way to contribute was to "do your own thing." But this solution was as wrong as the organization men's had been. Very few of the people who believed that doing one's own thing would lead to contribution, self-fulfillment, and success achieved any of the three.

But still, there is no return to the old answer of doing what you are told or assigned to do. Knowledge workers in particular have to learn to ask a question that has not been asked before: What *should* my contribution be? To answer it, they must address three distinct elements: What does the situation require? Given my strengths, my way of performing, and my values, how can I make the greatest contribution to what needs to be done? And finally, What results have to be achieved to make a difference?

Consider the experience of a newly appointed hospital administrator. The hospital was big and prestigious, but it had been coasting on its reputation for 30 years. The new administrator decided that his contribution should be to establish a standard of excellence in one important area within two years. He chose to focus on the emergency room, which was big, visible, and sloppy. He decided that every patient who came into the ER had to be seen by a qualified nurse within 60 seconds. Within 12 months, the hospital's emergency room had become a model for all hospitals in the United States, and within another two years, the whole hospital had been transformed.

As this example suggests, it is rarely possible—or even particularly fruitful—to look too far ahead. A plan can usually cover no more than 18 months and still be reasonably clear and specific. So the question in most cases should be, Where and how can I achieve results that will make a difference within the next year and a half? The answer must balance several things. First, the results should be hard to achieve—they should require "stretching," to use the current buzzword. But also, they should be within reach. To aim at results that cannot be achieved—or that can be only under the most unlikely circumstances—is not being ambitious; it is being foolish. Second, the results should be meaningful. They should make a difference. Finally, results should be visible and, if at all possible, measurable. From this will come a course of action: what to do, where and how to start, and what goals and deadlines to set.

Responsibility for Relationships

Very few people work by themselves and achieve results by themselves—a few great artists, a few great scientists, a few great athletes. Most people work with others and are effective with other people. That is true whether they are members of an organization or independently employed. Managing yourself requires taking responsibility for relationships. This has two parts.

The first is to accept the fact that other people are as much individuals as you yourself are. They perversely insist on behaving like human beings. This means that they too have their strengths; they too have their ways of getting things done; they too have their values. To be effective, therefore, you have to know the strengths, the performance modes, and the values of your coworkers.

That sounds obvious, but few people pay attention to it. Typical is the person who was trained to write reports in his or her first assignment because that boss was a reader. Even if the next boss is a listener, the person goes on writing reports that, invariably, produce no results. Invariably the boss will think the employee is stupid, incompetent, and lazy, and he or she will fail. But that could have been avoided if the employee had only looked at the new boss and analyzed how *this* boss performs.

Bosses are neither a title on the organization chart nor a "function." They are individuals and are entitled to do their work in the way they do it best. It is incumbent on the people who work with them to observe them, to find out how they work, and to adapt themselves to what makes their bosses most effective. This, in fact, is the secret of "managing" the boss.

The same holds true for all your coworkers. Each works his or her way, not your way. And each is entitled to work in his or her way. What matters is whether they perform and what their values are. As for how they perform—each is likely to do it differently. The first secret of effectiveness is to understand the people you work with and depend on so that you can make use of their strengths, their ways of working, and their values. Working relationships are as much based on the people as they are on the work.

The second part of relationship responsibility is taking responsibility for communication. Whenever I, or any other consultant, start to work with an organization, the first thing I hear about are all the personality conflicts. Most of these arise from the fact that people do not know what other people are doing and how they do their work, or what contribution the other people are concentrating on and what results they expect. And the reason they do not know is that they have not asked and therefore have not been told.

This failure to ask reflects human stupidity less than it reflects human history. Until recently, it was unnecessary to tell any of these things to anybody. In the medieval city, everyone in a district plied the same trade. In the countryside, everyone in a valley planted the same crop as soon as the frost was out of the ground. Even those few people who did things that were not "common" worked alone, so they did not have to tell anyone what they were doing.

Today the great majority of people work with others who have different tasks and responsibilities. The marketing vice president may have come out of sales and know everything about sales, but she knows nothing about the things she has never done—pricing, advertising, packaging, and the like. So the people who do these things must make sure that the marketing vice president understands what they are trying to do, why they are trying to do it, how they are going to do it, and what results to expect.

If the marketing vice president does not understand what these high-grade knowledge specialists are doing, it is primarily their fault, not hers. They have not educated her. Conversely, it is the marketing vice president's responsibility to make sure that all of her coworkers understand how she looks at marketing: what her goals are, how she works, and what she expects of herself and of each one of them.

Even people who understand the importance of taking responsibility for relationships often do not communicate sufficiently with their associates. They are afraid of being thought presumptuous or inquisitive or stupid. They are wrong. Whenever someone goes to his or her associates and says, "This is what I am good at. This is how I work. These are my values. This is the contribution I plan to concentrate on and the results I should be expected to deliver," the response is always, "This is most helpful. But why didn't you tell me earlier?"

And one gets the same reaction—without exception, in my experience—if one continues by asking, "And what do I need to know about your strengths, how you perform, your values, and your proposed contribution?" In fact, knowledge workers should request this of everyone with whom they work, whether as subordinate, superior, colleague, or team member. And again, whenever this is done, the reaction is always, "Thanks for asking me. But why didn't you ask me earlier?"

Organizations are no longer built on force but on trust. The existence of trust between people does not necessarily mean that they like one another. It means that they understand one another. Taking responsibility for relationships is therefore an absolute necessity. It is a duty. Whether one is a member of the organization, a consultant to it, a supplier, or a distributor, one owes that responsibility to all one's coworkers: those whose work one depends on as well as those who depend on one's own work.

The Second Half of Your Life

When work for most people meant manual labor, there was no need to worry about the second half of your life. You simply kept on doing what you had always done. And if you were lucky enough to survive 40 years of hard work in the mill or on the railroad, you were quite happy to spend the rest of your life doing nothing. Today, however, most work is knowledge work, and knowledge workers are not "finished" after 40 years on the job, they are merely bored.

We hear a great deal of talk about the midlife crisis of the executive. It is mostly boredom. At 45, most executives have reached the peak of their business careers, and they know it. After 20 years of doing very much the same kind of work, they are very good at their jobs. But they are not learning or contributing or deriving challenge and satisfaction from the job. And yet they are still likely to face another 20 if not 25 years of work. That is why managing oneself increasingly leads one to begin a second career.

There are three ways to develop a second career. The first is actually to start one. Often this takes nothing more than moving from one kind of organization to another: the divisional controller in a large corporation, for instance, becomes the controller of a medium-sized hospital. But there are also growing numbers of people who move into different lines of work altogether: the business executive or government official who enters the ministry at 45, for instance;

or the midlevel manager who leaves corporate life after 20 years to attend law school and become a small-town attorney.

We will see many more second careers undertaken by people who have achieved modest success in their first jobs. Such people have substantial skills, and they know how to work. They need a community—the house is empty with the children gone—and they need income as well. But above all, they need challenge.

The second way to prepare for the second half of your life is to develop a parallel career. Many people who are very successful in their first careers stay in the work they have been doing, either on a full-time or part-time or consulting basis. But in addition, they create a parallel job, usually in a nonprofit organization, that takes another ten hours of work a week. They might take over the administration of their church, for instance, or the presidency of the local Girl Scouts council. They might run the battered women's shelter, work as a children's librarian for the local public library, sit on the school board, and so on.

Finally, there are the social entrepreneurs. These are usually people who have been very successful in their first careers. They love their work, but it no longer challenges them. In many cases they keep on doing what they have been doing all along but spend less and less of their time on it. They also start another activity, usually a nonprofit. My friend Bob Buford, for example, built a very successful television company that he still runs. But he has also founded and built a successful nonprofit organization that works with Protestant churches, and he is building another to teach social entrepreneurs how to manage their own nonprofit ventures while still running their original businesses.

People who manage the second half of their lives may always be a minority. The majority may "retire on the job" and count the years until their actual retirement. But it is this minority, the men and women who see a long working-life expectancy as an opportunity both for themselves and for society, who will become leaders and models.

There is one prerequisite for managing the second half of your life: You must begin long before you enter it. When it first became clear 30 years ago that working-life expectancies were lengthening very fast, many observers (including myself) believed that retired people would increasingly become volunteers for nonprofit institutions. That has not happened. If one does not begin to volunteer before one is 40 or so, one will not volunteer once past 60.

Similarly, all the social entrepreneurs I know began to work in their chosen second enterprise long before they reached their peak in their original business. Consider the example of a successful lawyer, the legal counsel to a large corporation, who has started a venture to establish model schools in his state. He began to do volunteer legal work for the schools when he was around 35. He was elected to the school board at age 40. At age 50, when he had amassed a fortune, he started his own enterprise to build and to run model schools. He is, however, still working nearly full-time as the lead counsel in the company he helped found as a young lawyer.

There is another reason to develop a second major interest, and to develop it early. No one can expect to live very long without experiencing a serious setback in his or her life or work. There is the competent engineer who is passed over for promotion at age 45. There is the competent college professor who realizes at age 42 that she will never get a professorship at a big university, even though she may be fully qualified for it. There are tragedies in one's family life: the breakup of one's marriage or the loss of a child. At such times, a second major interest—not just a hobby—may make all the difference. The engineer, for example, now knows that he has not been very successful in his job. But in his outside activity—as church treasurer, for example—he is a success. One's family may break up, but in that outside activity there is still a community.

In a society in which success has become so terribly important, having options will become increasingly vital. Historically, there was no such thing as "success." The overwhelming majority of people did not expect anything but to stay in their "proper station," as an old English prayer has it. The only mobility was downward mobility.

In a knowledge society, however, we expect everyone to be a success. This is clearly an impossibility. For a great many people, there is at best an absence of failure. Wherever there is success, there has to be failure. And then it is vitally important for the individual, and equally for the individual's family, to have an area in which he or she can contribute, make a difference, and be *somebody*. That means finding a second area—whether in a second career, a parallel career, or a social venture—that offers an opportunity for being a leader, for being respected, for being a success.

The challenges of managing oneself may seem obvious, if not elementary. And the answers may seem self-evident to the point of appearing naïve. But managing oneself requires new and unprecedented things from the individual, and especially from the knowledge worker. In effect, managing oneself demands that each knowledge worker think and behave like a chief executive officer. Further, the shift from manual workers who do as they are told to knowledge workers who have to manage themselves profoundly challenges social structure. Every existing society, even the most individualistic one, takes two things for granted, if only subconsciously: that organizations outlive workers, and that most people stay put.

But today the opposite is true. Knowledge workers outlive organizations, and they are mobile. The need to manage oneself is therefore creating a revolution in human affairs.

Originally published in January 1999. Reprint R0501K

PETER F. DRUCKER was a writer, consultant, and professor of social science and management at Claremont Graduate University in California. His thirty-nine books have been published in more than seventy languages. He founded the Peter F. Drucker Foundation for Nonprofit Management, and counseled thirteen governments, public services institutions, and major corporations.

Index